DIGITAL IC
VESTPOCKET
HANDBOOK

Walter H. Buchsbaum, Sc.D.

PRENTICE-HALL, INC.

(Business and Professional Division)

ENGLEWOOD CLIFFS, NEW JERSEY

Prentice-Hall International, Inc., *London*
Prentice-Hall of Australia, Pty. Ltd., *Sydney*
Prentice-Hall of Canada, Ltd., *Toronto*
Prentice-Hall of India Private Ltd., *New Delhi*
Prentice-Hall of Japan, Inc., *Tokyo*
Prentice-Hall of Southeast Asia Pte. Ltd.,
  Singapore
Whitehall Books, Ltd., *Wellington, New
  Zealand*
Editoria Prentice-Hall do Brasil Ltda., *Rio de
  Janeiro*

© 1984 by
Prentice-Hall, Inc.
Englewood Cliffs, N.J.

Editor: George E. Parker

Library of Congress Cataloging in Publication Data

Buchsbaum, Walter H.
  Digital IC vestpocket handbook.

  Includes index.
  1. Integrated circuits—Handbook, manuals, etc.
I. Title. II. Title: Digital I.C. vestpocket handbook.
TK7874.B768 1984   621.381′73   83-13735
ISBN 0-13-212316-9

Printed in the United States of America

How to Use This Book

In today's world of electronics the single most widely used component is the integrated circuit and whenever logic or computing functions are performed, this IC is digital. Although there are thousands of type numbers, they can all be classified by function; even though they may contain thousands of transistors, their total function is usually defined by a few words, such as 64 K RAM, shift register, decoder, etc. To help you find your way through this maze of data, here is a book that provides all the information you need to understand, use, test and troubleshoot *all* types of digital ICs. The method we use here has proved successful in the widely used reference work "Encyclopedia of Integrated Circuits," and consists of a set of key data for each functional type of digital IC.

Each type of IC is listed by its function, regardless of size, IC family, voltage, speed or other characteristics. The listing for counters, for example, starts out with a general description of counter principles, illustrated by block diagrams, and then lists and explains the key parameters that apply specifically to counters. Next, we devote separate sections, all arranged in the same, uniform method, to each type of counter. Again, we classify counters by their function. We deal with synchronous and asynchronous counters, programmable, up/down counters, etc. In each section you will first find a brief description with a block diagram, key parameters with typical performance values for actual devices and a brief discussion of the application of these devices. Where appropriate we have added comments to provide all the information you need.

Even experienced engineers and technicians inevitably forget some of the fundamentals of digital logic. For that reason the first chapter contains, in a concise, concentrated form, all of the fundamental concepts and formulas for logic circuits, binary arithmetic, Boolean algebra and key design techniques such as Karnaugh mapping and flow charting. The second chapter covers actual digital ICs according to functional groups. Again, the material is concentrated, but complete. Chapter 3 deals with memory ICs and Chapter 4 covers microprocessor and microcomputer ICs. Support functions for the microprocessor/computer ICs are covered in Chapter 5. The detailed index includes synonyms for some of the terms used in this book so that, should you be familiar with a name for a device or function that is not listed here under that name, you will be able to locate it anyway. The main purpose of this vestpocket handbook is to let you take the essential information you need with you, wherever you may be. Just like its large-size cousin, this handbook will not become obsolete because, although different IC type numbers constantly appear on the market, the functions covered in this book remain the same and the information remains just as correct as ever.

The topics of logic circuits, digital system design, microprocessors and microcomputers, memory systems, etc, are each covered in wide-ranging detail in a host of books. This vestpocket handbook, however, contains only the concentrated essence of this field, with a sharp focus on integrated circuits. It will help reinforce, and add to, some of the things you may have learned from larger books. In a real sense, it will be your own miniature, non-volatile, highly portable random access memory (RAM).

Walter H. Buchsbaum
July 1983

Books by Walter H. Buchsbaum

Complete Handbook of Practical Electronics Reference Data (1978)

Complete Guide to Digital Test Equipment (1977)

Encyclopedia of Integrated Circuits: A Practical Handbook of Essential Reference Data (1980)

Complete TV Servicing Handbook (1982)

Analog IC Vestpocket Handbook (1984)

Interface IC Vestpocket Handbook (1984)

TABLE OF CONTENTS

Chapter 1

Chapter One is intended to provide a reminder for those readers who may have forgotten some of the fundamentals of digital logic. This chapter is primarily concerned with fundamental definitions, basic functions of circuits, the rules of Boolean algebra, the basics of binary numbers and Karnaugh maps and flow charts. The information contained in this chapter is concise, short and designed to provide a quick reference rather than a detailed explanation.

1.1 FUNDAMENTALS OF DIGITAL LOGIC

The word "digital" is always associated with discrete steps, units of a given size or number, as opposed to "analog," which refers to continuous variations. Digital signals are usually pulses, while analog signals may represent the human voice (audio), light variations (video) or other physical phenomena. In digital logic, discrete signals, such as pulses or voltage levels, are manipulated to produce results in terms of discrete quantities, such as numbers. Relays and switches are the original digital

1

logic devices, and much of that terminology persists in today's solid state digital technology. The terms "switches" and "gates" are used interchangeably to refer to the logic elements. These devices can have only two states—they can have open or closed contacts. Two relays with contacts in series must both be energized to allow current to flow through their contacts. If the contacts are connected in parallel, either relay can control current flow. These are the concepts used in the two basic digital logic elements— the AND and OR circuits.

A simple diode AND circuit is shown, together with its logic symbol, in Figure 1.1. The various possible combinations of input and output signals are summarized in the "truth table," in terms of "0" and "1". For convenience, we designate a positive voltage as "1" and a ground or negative voltage as "0". This convention is called "positive logic," and the opposite, a positive voltage meaning "0" and a ground meaning "1", is called, appropriately enough, "negative logic." Looking at the truth table of Figure 1.1, it is apparent that a "1" output can only occur when both A *and* the B input are "1". This corresponds to the case where both relays must be energized, because their contacts are in series.

The second function is shown by the circuit, logic symbol and truth table of Figure 1.2. Here a "1" output will occur if either the A *or* B input, *or* both, are a "1". This case corresponds to the two relays having contacts in parallel. Energizing either relay, or both, will allow current to flow.

In the circuits shown so far, the input and output signals are of the same polarity, but if transistors are used instead of diodes,

2

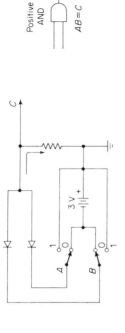

Figure 1.1. Diode AND circuit

M. Mandl, *Electronic Switching Circuits: Boolean Algebra and Mapping,* © 1969. Reprinted by permission of Prentice-Hall, Inc.

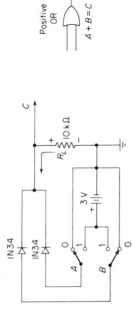

Truth Table		
A	B	C
0	0	0
1	0	1
0	1	1
1	1	1

$A + B = C$

Positive OR

Figure 1.2. Diode OR circuit

M. Mandl, Electronic Switching Circuits: Boolean Algebra and Mapping, © 1969. Reprinted by permission of Prentice-Hall, Inc.

4

it is possible to invert the polarity and perform the logic function in a single stage. It is therefore simple to change the AND circuit into a circuit in which there is a "1" output only when both inputs are *not* "1". Since this circuit, shown in Figure 1.3 with its truth table and symbol, has an output only in the NOT AND condition, it is called the *NAND* circuit.

Applying the same reasoning to the OR circuit, it is possible to obtain the NOT OR or *NOR* circuit, shown with its truth table and symbol in Figure 1.4.

By combining the basic AND and OR circuits with inverting functions, it is possible to obtain the NAND and the NOR logic element. By further combining these logic elements, it is possible to make up a very large variety of logic functions which can ultimately perform extremely complex computations, data processing and digital control tasks.

Digital logic elements usually operate in rapid sequence, with pulse trains as input and output signals. In order to provide some means of storing information, or delaying portions of the signal, it is possible to connect two gates (either NOR or NAND) in the circuit shown in Figure 1.5 to produce a "flip-flop" or multivibrator. Multivibrator circuits are described in Chapter 2. For digital logic applications, the circuit of Figure 1.5 acts as a toggle switch which can be set to two different positions by the input signal. If the input to R (Reset) is unchanged when the input to S (Set) changes, the polarity at both output leads will change. If both inputs change in the same way (both positive or both negative) at exactly the

Truth Table		
A	B	C
0	0	1
1	0	1
0	1	1
1	1	0

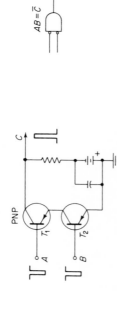

$AB = \bar{C}$

Figure 1.3. Transistor NAND circuit

M. Mandl, Electronic Switching Circuits: Boolean Algebra and Mapping, © 1969.
Reprinted by permission of Prentice-Hall, Inc.

6

$A + B = \bar{C}$

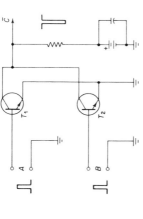

Figure 1.4. **Transistor NOR circuit**

M. Mandl, *Electronic Switching Circuits: Boolean Algebra and Mapping,* © 1969.
Reprinted by permission of Prentice-Hall, Inc.

Truth Table		
A	B	C
0	0	1
1	0	0
0	1	0
1	1	0

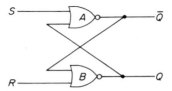

Figure 1.5.   RS flip-flop circuit

T. Sifferlen and V. Vartanian, Digital Electronics with Engineering Applications, © 1970. Reprinted by permission of Prentice-Hall, Inc.

same time, the output will not change. In logic applications, there are a number of combinations of flip-flops and logic gates to provide different functions. Flip-flops are represented symbolically by a rectangle with the input and output leads labeled.

A typical combination of flip-flop and gates is shown in Figure 1.6, in which a pulse train or "clock" changes the flip-flop according to the "0" or "1" condition of the S and R inputs. When a set of such flip-flops is connected as shown in Figure 1-7, a "binary" counter is obtained. As successive pulses enter into the first trigger or "clock" input, the "0" or "1" condition of the flip-flops change. Binary arithmetic is described in a later section.

The binary counter shown in Figure 1-7 can be used in a variety of ways. Each flip-flop (FF) stage can act to divide the number of pulses by two, because only the rising part of the pulse can change its state. That means two successive pulses are needed to

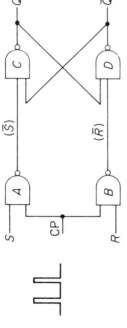

Figure 1.6. Clocked flip-flop circuit

T. Sifferlen and V. Vartanian, *Digital Electronics with Engineering Applications,* © 1970.
Reprinted by permission of Prentice-Hall, Inc.

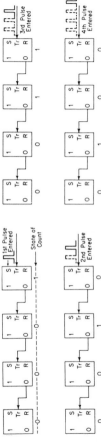

Figure 1.7. Binary counter operation

M. Mandl, Electronic Switching Circuits: Boolean Algebra and Mapping. © 1969. Reprinted by permission of Prentice-Hall, Inc.

produce one complete output pulse. When used in this manner, the binary counter becomes a binary divider. Two stages divide by four, three stages divide by eight and so on.

With the addition of AND gates a chain of FFs can become a shift register, as illustrated in Figure 1.8. A data signal is applied at the set input of the first FF, together with the clock signal. At the same time the inverse data signal, together with the clock signal, is applied to the reset input. As the clock signal pulses progress, the data signal is shifted, step-by-step, into the FFs. At the end of the desired number of clock signals, eight in this example, the data is contained in eight FFs (only three are shown in Figure 1.8). It is possible to stop and restart the shifting process at a later time, using the shift register as temporary storage for the data signal. It is also possible to obtain a parallel output of the data by connecting to the Q terminals of the FFs.

Shift registers can be obtained which can enter data in the parallel mode and read them out serially. By proper gating it is possible to shift in both directions, obtain the complement of a data train (connecting to the Q terminals) and recirculate the data repeatedly through the shift register. In real life applications a variety of shift registers are obtainable with large scale integrated (LSI) devices that perform essential functions in computers and other digital systems.

The basic shift register, in a special arrangement, is also used in Random Access Memories (RAM) and Read Only Memories (ROM) which are described in Chapter 3.

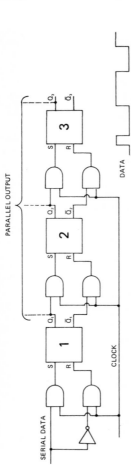

Figure 1.8. Simple shift register

Walter H. Buchsbaum, *Complete Guide to Digital Test Equipment*, © 1977.
Reprinted by permission of Prentice-Hall, Inc.

12

LSI devices are available which combine specific logic functions, starting from Binary-to-Decimal converters up to complete microcomputers. Figure 1.9 shows a widely used Binary-Coded-Decimal (BCD) to Decimal converter, with all of the logic contained in a single chip. Another LSI is shown in Figure 1.10. This device converts BCD numbers to the seven-segment format necessary to drive numerical displays. Note that in this device a relatively large number of gates are used, followed by seven transistor driver stages. Provision for lamp test (LT) and multiplexed driving power is included in this chip. Chapter 2 covers the display applications served by such devices.

STANDARD LOGIC SYMBOLS AND FUNCTIONS

MIL-STD 806B "Graphic Symbols for Logic Diagrams" is probably the most widely accepted standard because the Department of Defense has been the largest customer of digital devices. The MIL-STD logic symbols define the logic functions to be performed rather than the electronic circuit and are therefore equally applicable for positive and negative logic.

In positive logic, the positive voltage level at the inputs is defined as a "ONE" and the negative voltage level is defined as a "ZERO." In negative logic, the negative voltage level at the inputs is defined as a "ONE" while the positive level is defined as a "ZERO." The logic functions along with symbols are shown in Table 1.1. (Page 17)

The lines entering or leaving the symbols are the signal flow lines. A line entering

13

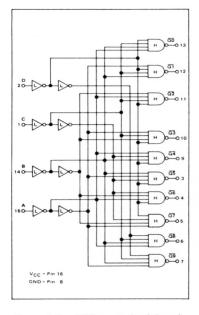

Figure 1.9.   BCD-to-decimal decoder

Walter H. Buchsbaum, Complete Guide to Digital Test Equipment, © 1977. Reprinted by permission of Prentice-Hall, Inc. Illustration courtesy of Motorola Semiconductor Products Div.

TRUTH TABLE

INPUT				OUTPUT									
D	C	B	A	0	1	2	3	4	5	6	7	8	9
0	0	0	0	0	1	1	1	1	1	1	1	1	1
0	0	0	1	1	0	1	1	1	1	1	1	1	1
0	0	1	0	1	1	0	1	1	1	1	1	1	1
0	0	1	1	1	1	1	0	1	1	1	1	1	1
0	1	0	0	1	1	1	1	0	1	1	1	1	1
0	1	0	1	1	1	1	1	1	0	1	1	1	1
0	1	1	0	1	1	1	1	1	1	0	1	1	1
0	1	1	1	1	1	1	1	1	1	1	0	1	1
1	0	0	0	1	1	1	1	1	1	1	1	0	1
1	0	0	1	1	1	1	1	1	1	1	1	1	0
1	0	1	0	1	1	1	1	1	1	1	1	1	1
1	0	1	1	1	1	1	1	1	1	1	1	1	1
1	1	0	0	1	1	1	1	1	1	1	1	1	1
1	1	0	1	1	1	1	1	1	1	1	1	1	1
1	1	1	0	1	1	1	1	1	1	1	1	1	1
1	1	1	1	1	1	1	1	1	1	1	1	1	1

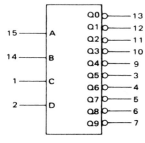

Input Loading Factor = 1
Output Loading Factor = 10
Total Power Dissipation = 125 mW typ/pkg
Propagation Delay Time = 22 ns typ

Figure 1.9 (Continued)

15

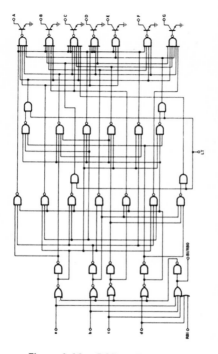

Figure 1.10. BCD-to-7-segment decoder and driver

Walter H. Buchsbaum, Complete Guide to Digital Equipment, © 1977. *Reprinted by permission of Prentice-Hall, Inc. Illustration courtesy of Signetics.*

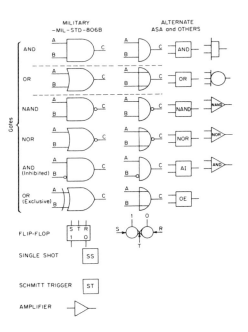

Table 1.1. Logic functions and symbols

Harry E. Thomas, Handbook of Transistors, Semiconductors, Instruments, and Microelectronics, © 1968. Reprinted by permission of Prentice-Hall, Inc.

17

or leaving a circle indicates a "low" signal level; a plain line indicates a "high" signal level. The symbols are defined for the AC-TIVE state of the device.

NUMBERING SYSTEMS

All modern numbering systems are mathematically constructed in identical fashion in that they have a base number where powers are used to provide increments of magnitude. For example in the 10 or decimal system, the number $32,684_{10}$ is made up of:

$$3 \times 10^4 + 2 \times 10^3 + 6 \times 10^2 + 8 \times 10 + 4 \times 1$$

$$
\begin{array}{llll}
\text{or} & 4 \times 10^0 & 4 \times 1 & = & 4 \\
& 8 \times 10^1 & 8 \times 10 & = + & 80 \\
& 6 \times 10^2 & 6 \times 100 & = + & 600 \\
& 2 \times 10^3 & 2 \times 1000 & = + & 2,000 \\
& 3 \times 10^4 & 3 \times 10,000 & = + & 30,000 \\
& \text{Total} & & & 32,684_{10}
\end{array}
$$

In the binary system, the base n = 2 is used to form any number by assigning fixed positions to each power of 2. For example:

	2^4	2^3	2^2	2^1	2^0
	16	8	4	2	1
Where	1	1	0	0	1

is summed up as follows

$$
\begin{array}{rcl}
1 \times 2^0 & = & 1 \\
0 \times 2^1 & = & 0 \\
0 \times 2^2 & = & 0
\end{array}
$$

$$1 \times 2^3 = 8$$
$$1 \times 2^4 = \underline{16}$$
$$\text{Total } 25_2$$

Table 1.2 lists the binary equivalents of decimal numbers for converting numbers from decimal to binary. (Page 20)

BINARY ARITHMETIC

Binary arithmetic follows the same rules as those used for decimal arithmetic. The basic functions of addition, subtraction, multiplication and division are still performed, but digital circuits perform these arithmetic operations in binary forms, instead of using the paper and pencil method people have learned for the decimal system.

The basic function in any arithmetic is addition, with subtraction the inverse of addition. Multiplication can be considered a series of successive additions. The product of 5 times 4 really means "what is the sum of 5 added to itself 4 times?" Division is the inverse of multiplication and can be considered as "how many times can one number be subtracted from another?" If we look at $12/3 = (12 - 3) - (3) - (3) = (3)$ we see that four successive subtractions are performed, and the answer is 4.

In binary arithmetic, the subtraction function can be performed by a form of addition. There are two techniques for performing this operation and both require "complementing" the number to be subtracted. The complement of a binary number is obtained by changing all "1's" to "0's"

Decimal number	Binary number
0	0
1	1
2	10
3	11
4	100
5	101
6	110
7	111
8	1000
9	1001
10	1010
11	1011
12	1100
13	1101
14	1110
15	1111
16	10000
17	10001
18	10010
19	10011
20	10100
21	10101
22	10110
23	10111
24	11000
25	11001
26	11010
27	11011
28	11100
29	11101
30	11110
31	11111
32	100000
33	100001
AND SO ON	

Table 1.2.   Binary equivalent numbers

and all "0's" to "1's". The complement of 11001 (25) is 00110 (6). Note that 11111 equals 31, which is also the sum of 25 + 6.

In the 2's complement method, 1 is added to the complement of the subtrahend, (number being subtracted) and the minuend (number being subtracted from) is then added to it.

Example: $15 - 9 = +6$;

$$
\begin{array}{r}
01111 \ (15) \\
- \ 10111 \ \text{(2's complement of 9)} \\
\hline
100110 \ \text{sum}
\end{array}
$$

$01001 = 9$

$10110 = $ complement of 9

$10110 + 1 = 10111 = $ 2's complement of 9

Since the sixth digit to the left above is a 1, the difference is positive and the resulting difference is $(+00110) = +6$. If the $n + 1$ digit (n = number of digits in the minuend) had been a zero, then the answer is negative and equal to the 2's complement of the sum.

The 1's complement method works in a similar manner. The subtrahend is complemented and the minuend is added to the subtrahend's complement. If the $n - 1$ position is 1, the difference is positive and 1 is added to the sum to get the correct difference. This operation is termed an "end-around carry." Example:

to subtract $8 - 6 = 2$ $0110 = 6$

$$
\begin{array}{r}
1000 = 8 \\
+ \ 1001 \quad \text{(1's complement of 6)} \\
\hline
10001 \\
+ \ 1 \\
\hline
10010 \rightarrow 0010 = +2
\end{array}
$$

If the sum has a 0 in the $n + 1$ digit position, the difference is negative and the correct answer is found by complementing the sum.

The 1's complement with "end-around carry" is more commonly used than the 2's complement.

Multiplication and division operations are performed as a continuous series of addition and subtraction operations. Detailed explanations of binary arithmetic are found in the references at the end of this chapter.

FUNDAMENTALS OF BOOLEAN ALGEBRA

Boolean algebra, originated by George Boole (1815-1864), set symbolic logic into mathematical form. It is presently taught as the algebra of sets, as compared to the more common algebra of fields, and is based on the following postulates:

AND	OR	NOT (complement)
$0 \cdot 0 = 0$	$0 + 0 = 0$	$\overline{1} = 0$
$0 \cdot 1 = 0$	$0 + 1 = 1$	$\overline{0} = 1$
$1 \cdot 0 = 0$	$1 + 0 = 1$	
$1 \cdot 1 = 1$	$1 + 1 = 1$	

BOOLEAN AXIOMS

A, B, C, etc. represent variables, each of which is a literal symbol. The complement of a variable is represented by $\overline{A}$, $\overline{B}$, $\overline{C}$.

Variables can only have values of 1 or 0; therefore, proofs become simple.

The symbols + (OR) imply ADDITION and · (AND) imply MULTIPLICATION.

Identity Laws (ONE and ZERO laws)

$$0 \cdot A = 0; \ 0 + A = A$$
$$1 \cdot A = A; \ 1 + A = 1$$

Commutative Law

$$A + B = B + A; \ A \cdot B = B \cdot A$$

Associative Law

$$A + (B + C) = (A + B) + C; \ A(BC) = (AB)C$$

The order of the numbers does not change the result. These laws are the same as in algebra.

Distributive Law (1)

$$A (B + C) = A \cdot B + A \cdot C.$$

Same as in algebra. Multiplying the sum of two variables by another variable is the same as multiplying each by the third and adding the sum.

Distributive Law (2)

$$A + (B \cdot C) = (A + C) \cdot (A + C)$$

New for Boolean algebra. Adding a variable to the product of two variables is the same as multiplying the sum of the first and second by the sum of the first and third.

Absorption Law

$$A + AB = A \quad A(A + B) = A$$

New for Boolean Algebra.

$$A + \overline{A}B = (A + B)$$

Since all variables can have only two values, "1" or "0", the above relationships hold true.

Complementary Law

$$A + \overline{A} = 1 \quad A \cdot \overline{A} = 0$$

New for Boolean algebra. A variable can have only two values, "1" or "0", and only one state can exist at a time; therefore, the above law holds true from the first postulates.

Indempotence Law

$$A + A = A \quad A \cdot A = A$$

New for Boolean algebra. In Boolean algebra there are no exponents (where $A \cdot A$ results in A^2), and the values are confined to "1" and "0". For this condition, the law is true. This law can be demonstrated using switching logic. If $A \cdot A$ are two switches in series, each has the same circuit; when one is closed, the other is closed. The two can be replaced with one. If $A + A$ are two switches in parallel, each having the same circuit, when one is closed the other is also closed. The two can be replaced by one.

De Morgan's Theorem

$$\overline{(A + B)} = \overline{A} \cdot \overline{B} \quad \overline{A \cdot B} = \overline{A} + \overline{B}$$

New for Boolean algebra. The complement of a sum of N variables is equal to the product of the separate variables' complement. The complement of a product of n variables is equal to the sum of the separate variables' complement.

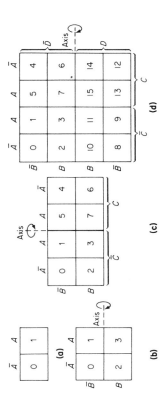

Figure 1.11. Karnaugh Map construction

T. Sifferlen and V. Vartanian, *Digital Electronics with Engineering Applications,* © 1970. Reprinted by permission of Prentice-Hall, Inc.

PRINCIPLES OF KARNAUGH MAPS

A multivariable function can be reduced to minimum form by the use of the Boolean Algebra laws stated above; however, for more than three variables, it is simpler to visualize and manipulate the logic by the use of a Karnaugh Map. A Karnaugh Map allocates a position for all of the truth table possibilities.

Figure 1.11 shows the buildup of the Karnaugh Map. A single variable has two states, ONE and ZERO. This is shown in Figure 1.11a. The ZERO state is labeled $\overline{A}$ and the ONE state is labeled A. The map contains a cell (square) for each of the states of the variable. A two variable map is generated by folding down the one variable map as shown in Figure 1.11. The folding is indicated by the axis, and the second variable becomes a mirror image of the first. A three variable map is generated by folding the two variable map along the axis shown in Figure 1.11c. The increase of the map is always twice its size, so that any map has 2^n cells where n is equal to the number of variables. The three variable map, for example, has 8 cells; $2^3 = 8$. The original cells are represented by $\overline{C}$ and the new cells by C. The four variable map is obtained by folding down the three variable map along the axis as shown in Figure 1.11. An examination of the maps developed, shows the following relationships:

(1) Going from one cell to an adjacent cell, only one variable changes. This is true going horizontally or vertically. It also holds true for a move-

26

ment from one end cell to the other end cell in the same row or column.

(2) The vertical outside columns of the map can be placed next to each other without affecting the map.

(3) In like manner, the horizontal outside rows of the map can be placed next to each other without affecting the map.

(4) Each time the map is enlarged, the original cells are the NOT portion of the new variable and the new cells are the TRUE portion of the new variable.

(5) Adjacent cells form a couple, which eliminates one variable in the function.

(6) In enlarging the map, the numerical representation of the new cells is obtained by adding 2^{n-1}, where n = number of variables in the map to the corresponding cells. In the four variable map, the new cells are numerically represented by adding 8 ($2^{4-1} = 2^3 = 8$) to the corresponding cells of the three variable map.

(7) The true values of the variables from a truth table are entered in the proper squares of the map as "1". The false values are entered as a "0".

(8) All adjacent "1's" are circled in groups of powers of 2; i.e.—2, 4, 8, etc.

USING THE KARNAUGH MAP

Figure 1.12 is the map of

$$F = A\overline{B}C + \overline{A}\overline{B}C + AB\overline{D}$$
$$+ \overline{A}B\overline{C} + BC\overline{D} + BCD$$

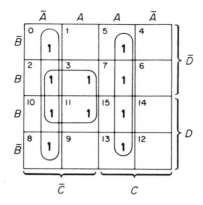

Figure 1.12. Use of Karnaugh Map

T. Sifferlen and V. Vartanian, Digital Electronics with Engineering Applications, © 1970. Reprinted by permission of Prentice-Hall, Inc.

Three quadruples (group of four adjacent "1's") can be formed. (Note: The cells of numerals 7 and 15 could have been joined with 3 and 11 instead of 6 and 14 for solution.) The selection is left to the designer, based upon which signals are available. The function is reduced to

$$F = A\overline{C} + \overline{A}C + BC = C(\overline{A} + B) + A\overline{C}.$$

The map also represents those functions which have a "0" marked in them. The NOT function could be determined for these:

28

$$F = \overline{\overline{AC} + A\overline{BC}}$$

The designer, in some cases, may find this easier to implement, particularly if using NOR logic gates.

Logic network functions can be categorized as one of the two types, either a "Product of Sums" or a "Sum of Products."

A Karnaugh Map generates a sum of products logic network, that is, a group of ANDed functions being summed or ORed to give a single function output.

1.2 FUNDAMENTALS OF LOGIC DESIGN

BASIC FLOW CHARTING

Flow charting is a technique used in various phases of digital logic and computer design, and is generally used at the following levels:

1. Circuit design analysis.
2. System signal flow.
3. Computer program design. (Same level as system signal flow.)

CIRCUIT FLOW CHARTING

Logic systems are made up of large numbers of sequentially operating circuits, and the outputs of these circuits are functions of both present and past input signals. These input signals may be external signals

29

or internal feedback or loop signals. Timing diagrams are used to show the sequence of operation, but timing diagrams do not represent the circuit operations for different input sequences. Just like individual circuits, whole networks have stable and unstable states. The stable state is shown in the truth tables, as described in the previous pages. The unstable state occurs normally during the transient or transitional period between two stable states as a result of an input signal. The unstable states can cause race conditions and "false" inputs to other circuits.

Circuit flow charting utilizes the Karnaugh Map to diagrammatically show all of the possible output states for all of the input signals. There are seven basic steps to network analysis by flow chart.

1. Label all of the gates (AND, OR, NOR, etc.) that make up the network in some appropriate manner (by decimal, number, letter, etc.).
2. Write the Boolean expression for the output of each of these gates. This is done from the immediate inputs of the gate.
3. Draw the flow chart, which looks the same as a Karnaugh Map, using one column for each external input and one for each internal input combination.
4. Enter the Boolean expression for the output of gate 1 to the left of each column using the Karnaugh Map as a chart.
5. Enter the Boolean expression for the output of the rest of the gates to the

right of gate 1, in proper sequence, the highest gate number farthest to the right.

6. Identify the stable and non-stable states. When the binary number within the square is equal to the binary number labeling the row, the state is stable, all others are unstable.

7. To go from one stable state to another, requires going through all unstable states. The binary number within the square indicates the row to which the operating point will move. The movement stays within the same column since it is assumed that the external inputs have not changed during this time. The movement of the operating point is depicted by arrows going from one state to another.

SYSTEM SIGNAL FLOW CHARTING

System signal flow charting uses some of the same symbols used in computer system flow charting, as shown in Figure 1.13. Flow charting lists the sequence of events to be performed, step-by-step, to complete a function.

For example: Multiply two 4-bit numbers ($5 \times 7 = 35$).

$$
\begin{array}{r}
0101 = 5 \\
\times \quad 0111 = 7 \\
\hline
0100011 = 35
\end{array}
$$

To perform the multiplication requires the use of four registers: Register A—Multiplicand (number being multiplied) Register;

31

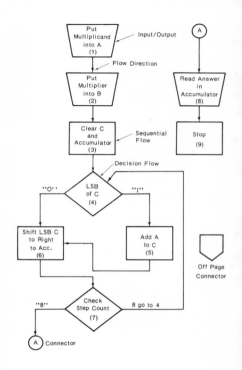

Figure 1.13.   Flow chart of a multiplication

Register B—Adding Register; Register C—
Multiplier Register and an Accumulator
Register for the answer. Multiplication is
performed by successive addition and shifting. Writing out the sequence of events:

1. Put Multiplicand into Register A.
2. Put Multiplier into Register C.
3. Clear Register B.
4. Clear Accumulator Register.
5. Look at Least Significant Bit (LSB)
   of C.
6. If zero, shift LSB of B to Accumulator.
7. If 1, Add A to C and put sum in B.
8. Shift LSB of B to Accumulator.
9. Shift Register C 1 bit.
10. Look at LSB of C.
11. If zero, shift LSB of B to Accumu-
    lator C.
12. If one, add A to C and put sum in B.
13. Shift LSB of B to Accumulator.
14. Repeat 5.

The flow chart of Figure 1.13 explains
the previous steps in a pictorial form. Note
that only three different "action" symbols
(Input/Output, Decision and Sequential
Flow) are required to describe all steps.

SYNCHRONOUS AND
ASYNCHRONOUS LOGIC SYSTEMS

A synchronous logic system operates
from a fixed time source (clock), and all
operations are related (or synchronized) to
some sub-multiple of the source. A synchronous system runs continuously after being

started initially as the result of some external action. The resulting sequence of events is in synchronism with the starting event. Synchronous systems are easier to design and implement since all operation occurrences are assigned a unique time period within the sequence.

Asynchronous systems have operations occurring in apparently random fashion, since the controlling factor is the function to be performed. Asynchronous operation allows for greater flexibility and a savings in hardware and system cycle time, though such systems are more difficult to design. Asynchronous systems are the result of a large number of random timed inputs of varying length and frequency.

Synchronous systems with multiple inputs poll or multiplex the inputs. In these systems, each input is polled in its proper turn; if information is available, it is acted upon before going on to the next input line. Asynchronous systems utilize a technique of "First in, First out," (FIFO) whereby the input advises the system that it has information.

Chapter 2

Chapter Two covers those digital ICs which form the building blocks of most larger digital systems. The most basic and widely used circuits are covered here in sufficient detail to allow the reader to deal with any of the variations he may encounter in the field. Beginning with the basic logic gates and briefly covering multiple gates, arrays and expanders, we go on to the basic flip-flop, its variations, including the monostable multivibrator and the application of flip-flops as shift registers of various types. Other essential building blocks in any digital system are the various buffers, inverters, line drivers and receivers. All basic types of counters and decoders/encoders as well as display driver ICs are also included. The chapter concludes with the fundamental arithmetic functions, as they are provided by individual ICs.

2.1 GATES, LOGIC

DESCRIPTION

The six basic logic gates illustrated in Figure 2.1 form the building blocks of al-

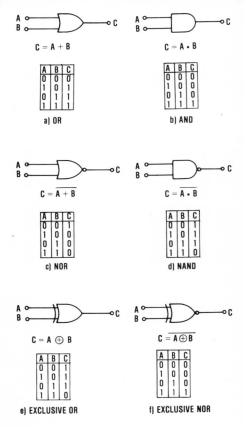

Figure 2.1. (a) OR
(b) AND
(c) NOR
(d) NAND
(e) Exclusive OR
(f) Exclusive NOR

most all digital functions provided in ICs. Practically all digital medium and large-scale integrated circuits contain these fundamental logic gates, and a large variety of specific gate function arrays are available in every digital IC family.

Figure 2.1(a) illustrates the two-input OR circuit, its Boolean function and its truth table. Figure (c) shows the same symbol with a circle at the output, indicating the complementing or inverting function, the NOR circuit. Figures 2.1(b) and (d) illustrate the AND and the NAND circuits, respectively. The Exclusive OR and the Exclusive NOR circuits, as shown in Figures 2.1(e) and (f), together with their Boolean notation and truth table, comprise special applications of the OR and NOR function.

While the Boolean equations of each of the six logic gates illustrated in Figure 2.1 are different, the truth tables of some of them are identical. Note, for example, that the truth table of the NAND circuit is identical to the truth table of the exclusive OR. The truth table of the AND circuit is identical to the exclusive NOR circuit. This implies that in many cases these circuits can be used interchangeably. Boolean algebra is covered in Chapter 1.

KEY PARAMETERS

a) *Propagation delay time*. The time required between input and output. This parameter depends on the particular digital IC family.
b) *Input loading factor*. The voltage and/or current required for each in-

put. This depends largely on the particular digital IC family.

c) *Output loading (fan-out)*. The output capability of each terminal, stated as either current source or sink, or as number of input loads. This parameter depends largely on the particular digital IC family.

APPLICATIONS

Logic gates are the building blocks of all digital ICs and are used in all digital systems.

COMMENTS

Because logic gates are so important, a large assortment of gate ICs are available in each digital IC family. Only a few representative examples are included here.

2.2 GATES, MULTIPLE

DESCRIPTION

The most widely used package in all digital IC families is the DIP configuration with 16 terminals. The three multiple gate arrangements shown in Figure 2.2 illustrate the most popular multiple gate configurations. Every digital IC family provides at least these three configurations as well as a number of specialized ones. There are quad 2-input OR, AND, NAND, NOR, and exclusive ORs available, as well as triple 3-input and dual 4-input gates of all types. There is

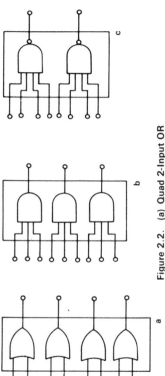

Figure 2.2.   (a) Quad 2-Input OR
               (b) Triple 3-Input AND
               (c) Dual 4-Input NAND

39

also a single 8-input gate type, usually as AND or NAND configurations. Variations of these standard configurations include the use of external pull-up resistors to provide interfacing with the desired voltage and current levels, or else output driver amplifiers are included to increase the output loading capability (fan-out).

KEY PARAMETERS

The key parameters described in Section 2.1 apply equally to the multiple gate ICs and must be referred to the particular digital IC families to obtain particular values.

APPLICATION

Multiple logic gate ICs are used as supplementary functions for large-scale integrated circuits on which the gates are part of the entire configuration. For small digital systems, the multiple gate ICs may be used to perform the required logic functions.

2.3 GATES, ARRAY

DESCRIPTION

A wide variety of logic gate arrays are available in ICs, some of which perform such frequently used functions as binary-to-BCD or BCD-to-7-segment display code conversions. The type of logic gate array described here can perform several different functions and therefore offers a very flexible logic assembly.

The gate array illustrated in Figure 2.3 can serve as a 4-bit AND/OR selector, and a quad 2-channel data selector, or as a quad exclusive NOR gate. There are eight data inputs, which are combined in NOR circuits with two control inputs, A and B. The output of each two NOR circuits is fed into an exclusive NOR circuit which is then controlled by the NAND circuits and the combination of inputs A and B. Note that each of the four data output lines contains an inverter to provide maximum output loading capability (fan-out).

KEY PARAMETERS

a) *Propagation delay time.* The time between input and output. 250 ns is typical as 5 V for low-power CMOS.
b) *Input loading.* For low-power CMOS, the input voltage at 5 V power supply is typically 2.5 V for **0** and at least 2.75 V for **1** logic level.
c) *Output loading capability (fan-out).* For low-power CMOS, the fan-out is in the order of 50. This means each output of Figure 2.3 can drive up to 50 inputs, equivalent to each of the data inputs of that same IC.

APPLICATIONS

This IC is used in a variety of digital systems to perform one of the following functions: 4-bit AND/OR selector, quad-2-channel data selector, or quad exclusive NOR gate array.

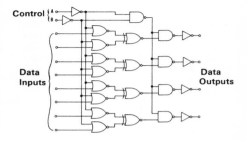

Figure 2.3. Logic Diagram—
Typical Gate Array

2.4 GATES, EXPANDABLE/ EXPANDER

DESCRIPTION

In some applications a relatively great number of inputs must be combined in the AND, OR, or other logic function. One method of increasing the number of inputs to a particular logic gate function is to use an expandable system, combined with an expander. Figure 2.4 illustrates two separate ICs, an expandable gate input, an AND circuit, and an 8-input AND expander which can be used with it. The expandable 8-input NAND circuit illustrated in Figure 2.4(a) consists of two 4-input AND circuits which drive a NOR circuit. The NOR has two special terminals, one for introducing the expansion signal X and the other for its complement, $\overline{X}$. The 8-input expander shown in Figure 2.4(b) consists of two 4-input circuits with a special output for the complement of the AND gate. To obtain a 16-input NAND function, the expander outputs are simply connected to the corresponding inputs of the expandable 8-input AND circuit. The terminals marked X are connected together, as are those marked $\overline{X}$.

KEY PARAMETERS

a) *Propagation delay time*. The time required between input and output.

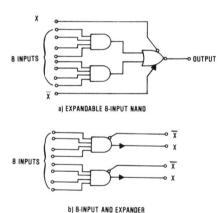

a) EXPANDABLE 8-INPUT NAND

b) 8-INPUT AND EXPANDER

Figure 2.4. (a) Expandable 8-Input
NAND
(b) 8-Input AND
Expander

43

18 ns is typical for TTL ICs, and 300 ns is typical for high-voltage CMOS ICs.

b) *Input loading.* The input voltage or current required for each pin on the IC. This depends on the particular digital IC family.

c) *Output loading capacity (fan-out).* The number of equivalent input circuits that can be connected to each output terminal. This depends largely on the particular digital IC family.

APPLICATIONS

In all digital systems where more than eight inputs must be combined in one of the logic gate functions.

2.5 FLIP-FLOPS (FF)

DESCRIPTION

One of the key building blocks of all digital logic systems, the flip-flop (FF) is available in a variety of different FF circuits with a host of different features.

As illustrated in Figure 2.5(a), the basic flip-flop consists of two gates with the appropriate cross connection. The actual circuitry of a D-type, positive edge triggered FF is shown in Figure 2.5(b), and illustrates the application of different gating circuits to the basic FF function. Note the presence of the "clock," "reset" (clear), and "set" inputs in addition to the actual data input, terminal D. The logic level at input D is transferred to the Q output only during the positive going edge of the clock pulse. When the clock pulse is at either the **0** or the **1** level, the D input signal has no effect. The "set" input signal can set the condition of the FF any time, regardless of the presence or absence of a clock pulse. Similarly, the "reset" signal can restore the condition of the FF any time.

The detailed operation of the FF is summarized by the truth table of Figure 2.5(c). The set and reset (clear) operations can occur regardless of the presence of the clock pulse, but data inputs at terminal D can occur only during the positive edge of the clock pulse when the set and reset signals are **0**. If both set and clear signals are **1**, simultaneously, it is possible for both Q and Q signals to be **1** at the same time. The actual condition of the outputs is undetermined and unpredictable in this situation.

KEY PARAMETERS

a) *Maximum power dissipation*. The maximum power that the IC can dissipate over the specified temperature range, usually from −40 to +85° C.

b) *Quiescent current*. The current drawn when the FFs on the entire IC are not operating.

c) *Toggle rate*. The maximum frequency at which the FF can change state.

d) *Propagation delay, clock to output*. The time required from the clock pulse transition until a change takes place in the FF output terminal.

e) *Propagation delay, set or reset to output*. The time delay from the ap-

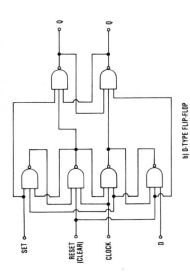

Figure 2.5. (a) Basic Flip-Flop
(b) D-Type Flip-Flop

46

CLOCK	DATA	RESET	SET	Q	Q̄
⟋	0	0	0	0	1
⟋	1	0	0	1	0
⟍	X	0	0	NC	NC
X	X	1	0	0	1
X	X	0	1	1	0
X	X	1	1	1	1

c) TRUTH TABLE   X—DON'T CARE
                        NC—NO CHANGE

Figure 2.5. (c) Truth Table

plication of the set or reset signal
until the output state changes.

f) *Clock pulse width.* The minimum
width of the clock pulse required for
reliable operation.

g) *Set or reset pulse width.* The minimum width of the set or reset pulse.

APPLICATIONS

FFs of every type are found in IC applications such as counters, shift registers,
microprocessors, memories, etc. ICs containing a small number of FFs on which
all terminals are available are used as
auxiliary circuits in digital systems. FFs
are used as short-time delays, set-reset
switches, and in a host of other control
applications.

COMMENTS

FFs are available in every digital logic
IC family and can be obtained in a wide

47

variety of characteristics and operational features. The following pages highlight the most frequently used specific FF ICs.

2.6 FLIP-FLOP, DUAL-TYPE D

DESCRIPTION

This universally used flip-flop (FF) contains two separate type D FFs, as illustrated in the functional diagram of Figure 2.6. Each of the two FFs is identical and can be used separately or interconnected with each other for whatever purpose may be required. They can be used as shift register elements or as type D FFs for counter or toggle applications.

KEY PARAMETERS

a) *Quiescent current.* The current drawn by the IC when no operations take place. 2.0 nA are typical at 5 V for low-power CMOS.

b) *Toggle rate.* The frequency with which the FF can change state. 4.0 MHz is typical for low-power CMOS and up to 50 MHz is typical for low-power TTL ICs.

c) *Propagation delay, clock to output.* The time required from the clock pulse transition until a change occurs in the output terminal. 175 ns is typical for low-power CMOS and 10 ns is typical for low-power TTL ICs.

d) *Propagation delay, set or reset to output.* The time required for either the set or reset signal to change the

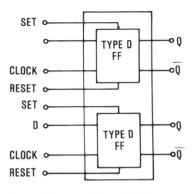

Figure 2.6. Dual Type D FF Function Block

output. 175 ns is typical for low-power CMOS and 13 ns is typical for low-power TTL ICs.

e) *Clock pulse width.* 250 ns is typical for low-power CMOS and 12 ns is typical for low-power TTL ICs.

2.7 FLIP-FLOP, DUAL J-K

DESCRIPTION

The J-K FF, and the type D FF described in the previous pages, are the most popular and widely used types of FFs. The main difference between them is that the J-K terminals replace the D-input.

As illustrated in the logic diagram of Figure 2.7(a), the J-K FF requires more logic

49

elements but also can perform different functions. The detailed functions available are summarized in the truth table of Figure 2.7(b). Note that where there were two possible data inputs in the type D-FF, there are four possible data inputs in the J-K type because either or both of these terminals can assume the 0 or the 1 state. In the truth table of the J-K FF the change from the present condition of Q to the next condition of the outputs is indicated, because the change rather than the static operation is the key function of the J-K FF.

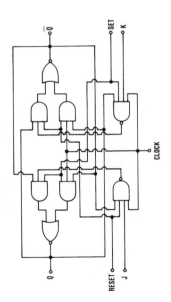

Figure 2.7. (a) Logic Diagram J-K Flip-Flop

| | | | | | PRESENT | NEXT | |
CLOCK	J	K	S	R	Q_1	Q	$\overline{Q}$
⤒	1	X	0	0	0	1	0
⤒	X	0	0	0	1	1	0
⤒	0	X	0	0	0	0	1
⤒	X	1	0	0	1	0	1
⤓	X	X	0	0	X	NC	NC
X	X	X	1	0	X	1	0
X	X	X	0	1	X	0	1
X	X	X	1	1	X	1	1

X—DON'T CARE
NC—NO CHANGE

Figure 2.7.   (b) Truth Table

KEY PARAMETERS

a) *Quiescent current.* The current drawn by the IC when no operations take place. 2.0 nA at 5 V is typical for low-power CMOS.

b) *Toggle rate.* The maximum frequency at which the FFs change state. 3 MHz is typical for low-power CMOS and 45 MHz is typical for low-power TTL ICs.

c) *Propagation delay, clock to output.* The time delay from the clock pulse transition to a change in the output. 175 ns is typical for low-power CMOS and 11 ns is typical for low-power TTL ICs.

d) *Propagation delay, set to output.* The time from the application of the set pulse until a change occurs at the output. 175 ns is typical for low-power

CMOS and 16 ns is typical for low-power TTL ICs.

e) *Propagation delay, reset to output.* The time required from the application of the reset signal until a change occurs at the output. 350 ns is typical for low-power CMOS and 16 ns is typical for low-power CMOS and 16 ns is typical for low-power TTL ICs.

f) *Clock pulse width.* 165 ns is typical for low-power CMOS and 12 ns is typical for low-power TTL ICs.

APPLICATIONS

J-K FFs are found in all digital equipment for control, register, or toggle functions.

COMMENTS

Although a dual J-K FF IC is described here, the number of J-K FFs that are available in a single IC depends only on the pin connections available. When common clock, set and reset controls are used, more than two J-K FFs can be made available on a 16-pin standard IC.

2.8 MULTIVIBRATOR, MONOSTABLE (ONE-SHOT)

DESCRIPTION

Multivibrators are a form of flip-flop circuit in which an R-C time constant is used to determine the rate of change of state

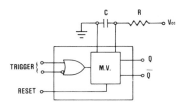

a) Monostable Multivibrator (One-Shot)

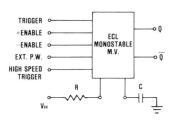

b) Function Block

Figure 2.8. (a) Monostable Multivibrator
(One-Shot)
(b) Function Block

(toggling). In the monostable or one-shot multivibrator (MV), an external trigger signal starts the change of the state of this MV and the external R-C time constant determines the time required from the beginning to the end of this one-shot oscillation.

53

A basic monostable MV is shown in Figure 2.8(a). The key elements are the two trigger inputs, the reset input, and the values of the external R-C time constant. Note that the OR circuit which triggers the MV has a small circle on one of its inputs, indicating that it can accept either a positive or a negative edge trigger. The edge-triggering ability is produced because this particular OR circuit is combined with a Schmitt-Trigger effect. In some ICs this type of circuit has a hysteresis characteristic and is referred to as "transmission gate."

The operation of the monostable MV requires that it be first reset so that the Q output is 0 and the $\overline{Q}$ is 1. When either a positive or a negative trigger signal is entered, the Q immediately changes to 1 and the $\overline{Q}$ to 0. After a period of time, determined by the R-C time constant, the MV returns to its original state, having generated one pulse. Whenever the reset signal occurs, the MV will return to the original state where Q is at 0. In retriggerable monostable MVs, any trigger signal that occurs during the period when Q is at 1 prolongs the duration of the pulse beond the time period determined by R-C.

The function logic (ECL) of a typical emitter-coupled logic (ECL) monostable MV is illustrated in Figure 2.8(b) and shows some of the various features that are available in monostable MV ICs. Trigger signals are applied to the trigger input and the external +enable or −enable signals determine whether the MV will accept positive or negative going edges. Internal Schmitt-Trigger circuits make the trigger input insensitive to rise and fall times. Although there is an external R-C time constant, there is also an input for external pulse-width control. With an external resistor, a control voltage can be used to vary the pulse width. When a control current is used, the resistor is not required. In addition, this ECL IC has a special "high-speed trigger" input which bypasses the internal Schmitt-Trigger circuits and permits a particularly rapid response.

Monostable MVs are available that can be retriggered during the pulse generation, with the number of the triggers that occur within a given time period increasing the pulse width according to a fixed ratio. Other monostable MVs include a preset feature which can be combined with retriggering to generate specific pulse waveforms.

KEY PARAMETERS

a) *Power dissipation.* 150 mW is typical of standard TTL ICs, 30 to 60 mW is typical of low-power TTL ICs, 250 mW is typical for low-power CMOS ICs, and 415 mW is typical for ECL ICs without any external load.

b) *Quiescent current.* The current drawn by the IC when no operations occur. 5.0 nA at 5 V is typical for low-power CMOS, 12 mA is typical for TTL, and 4.0 mA is typical for low-power TTL ICs.

c) *Propagation delay time, trigger input to change of output.* The time required from the trigger edge instant until an output change takes place. A typical value for ECL ICs is 4.0 ns and 2.0 ns at the high-speed trigger input. TTL and low-power TTL ICs have a time delay of approximately 40 to 50 ns. 300 ns is the typical value for low-power CMOS ICs at 5 V.

d) *Minimum input pulse width.* 2.0 ns is typical for ECL ICs, 40 to 50 ns is typical for standard or low-power TTL ICs, and 35 to 80 ns is typical for CMOS ICs at 5 V.

e) *Minimum reset pulse width.* 40 to 50 ns is typical for standard and low-power TTL ICs; 100 ns is typical for low-power CMOS ICs.

f) *Minimum output pulse reset time.* 1.5 ns is typical for ECL ICs, 10 to 15 ns is typical for standard and low-power TTL ICs, and 180 ns is typical for low-power CMOS at 5 V.

g) *Minimum output pulse fall time.* 1.5 ns is typical for ECL ICs, 10 to 20 ns is typical for standard and low-power TTL ICs, and 100 ns is typical for CMOS ICs at 5 V.

APPLICATIONS

Monostable MVs are used in a variety of timing circuits and wherever pulses of specific duration are required. They are found in a large variety of digital systems and form one of the building blocks in timing and sequencing sections.

COMMENTS

A variety of features can be combined in the basic monostable MV as described above. Many of the standard ICs contain two identical monostable MVs on a single package.

2.9 SHIFT REGISTER, STATIC

DESCRIPTION

Flip-flops (FF) can be connected as counters or shift registers as explained in Chapter 1. When used as a shift register, the FF functions as temporary memory or storage element, rather than the "divide-by-two" element used in counters. The basic shift register operation is described in Figure 2.9 which shows the logic diagram of a 4-bit static shift register and the truth table of that shift register during clocked operation. The data stream, a series of waves or pulses, is applied at the data input, where two inverters provide buffering and drive the D-input to the first FF. This FF will transfer the 0 or 1 condition present at the D-input only during that short period of time when the clock pulse edge rises. If a 1 is entered at D, this will appear as a 1 at the Q output. An inverter is used here as output buffer and it simply uses the $\overline{Q}$ signal to provide the correct Q output. During the next clock pulse rising edge, the 1 is transferred to the Q output of the second FF. During subsequent clock pulses, this 1 logic information, or bit, moves from left to right through each of the FFs. It takes four clock pulses to move a bit from the first FF to the last. Of course, other information, either 0

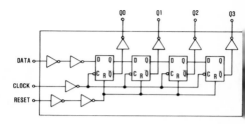

a) LOGIC DIAGRAM — 4-BIT STATIC SHIFT REGISTER

R	D	Q_n	Q_{n-1}
1	X	0	0
0	0	0	0
0	0	1	0
0	1	0	1
0	1	1	1

X—DON'T CARE

$Q_{n-1} = D_n$

b) TRUTH TABLE—CLOCKED OPERATION

Figure 2.9. (a) Logic Diagram—4-Bit Static Shift Register
(b) Truth Table—Clocked Operation

or 1, will appear at the D-terminal of the first FF and will move into the shift register.

If only four clock pulses are present, the four bits of information will be loaded into each of the four FFs and will appear as parallel data at the Q0, Q1, Q2 and Q3 output terminals. When a 1 signal appears at the reset terminal, all of the four FFs will change to 0 at their Q output. This is indicated in the first line of the truth table of Figure 2.9. Note that in this truth table the change from one data bit or one clock pulse to the next is indicated by the Q_n and Q_{n+1} columns.

A typical static register IC will contain two identical 4-bit registers on a single IC. The following pages describe shift registers that can shift both left to right and right to left, and can provide parallel input as well as output in a variety of combinations.

KEY PARAMETERS

a) *Power dissipation.* Either the maximum or the typical power dissipation of an entire IC is given.

b) *Quiescent current.* The current drawn by the IC when no operations take place.

c) *Toggle rate.* The highest clock frequency that can be used for this shift register.

d) *Output loading (fan-out).* The number of digital inputs that can be driven from a particular output without impairing the operation of the driver.

e) *Output rise time.* The time elapsed between 10% and 90% of the amplitude of the leading edge of the outset pulse.

APPLICATIONS

Shift registers are used throughout all digital systems to manipulate and rearrange digital data, to provide temporary storage of digital data, and to perform mathematical functions such as accumulation, comparison, etc.

2.10 SHIFT REGISTER, SERIAL-IN, PARALLEL-OUT— PARALLEL-IN/ SERIAL-OUT

DESCRIPTION

Two specific 8-bit shift register ICs are described and illustrated in Figure 2.10. In Figure 2.10(a) the partial logic diagram of a serial-in/parallel-out register is shown. Note that there are two data inputs, combined in an AND circuit. This permits gating or control of the data at terminal A through appropriate signals at terminal B. Eight identical FFs are contained in this IC, controlled by a common clock and a common reset signal.

The logic diagram of an 8-bit parallel-in/serial-out shift register is shown in Figure 2.10(b). Information is entered in parallel at the data inputs P1 through P8 which preset FFs 1 through 8. As clock pulses move the information from left to right, the output of the eight preset FFs will appear in serial form at the Q output terminal. It takes eight clock pulses, after each of the eight P-terminals has been set, to shift out this 8-bit byte of information.

In another mode of operation, this same shift register can enter data serially and output them serially. The parallel/serial terminal acts as a control and provides the gating for each FF. When the signal at that terminal is 0, the IC will operate with parallel input and serial output, but when that control terminal is 1, the IC will enter data serially and shift them out in the same manner. The simpler serial-in/par-

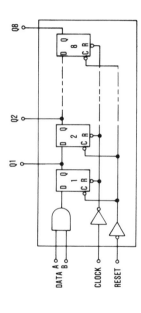

Figure 2.10. (a) Logic Diagram—8-Bit, Serial In/Parallel Out—Shift Register

61

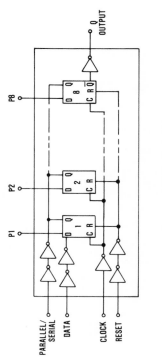

Figure 2.10. (b) Logic Diagram—8 Bit,
Parallel In/Serial Out—
Shift Register

allel-out shift register shown in Figure 2.10(a) does not have this control, but if only the Q8 output is used, it will automatically act as serial output.

KEY PARAMETERS

a) *Power dissipation.* Typical power dissipation is 120 mW for low-power TTL ICs, 300 mW for standard TTL ICs, and 350 mW for low-power CMOS ICs.

b) *Toggle rate.* The highest clock frequency for standard and low-power TTL ICs is 45 MHz. For CMOS ICs 2.0 MHz is typical at 5 V power supply.

c) *Propagation delay, clock-to-output.* 30 ns is typical for low-power TTL ICs.

d) *Propagation delay time, reset-to-output.* For low-power TTL ICs, 25 ns is typical.

e) *Clock pulse width.* 20 ns is typical for low-power TTL ICs.

f) *Reset pulse width.* 20 ns is typical for low-power TTL ICs.

APPLICATIONS

Used in all aspects of digital systems, these shift registers are particularly useful as parallel-to-serial, or serial-to-parallel converters.

COMMENTS

In some versions of these shift registers, special input or output terminals are pro-

63

vided for the first three or other selected FFs. Consult the manufacturer's data to meet specific requirements.

2.11 SHIFT REGISTER, 4-BIT UNIVERSAL

DESCRIPTION

This shift register can perform both serial and parallel input and output as well as left and right shift. Universal shift registers are available in all digital IC families and use the same basic R-S flip-flop (FF) as the simpler shift registers. Their ability to accept data in serial as well as parallel form, to provide both serial and parallel outputs, and to allow the data to be shifted either to the left or to the right, is due to a specific array of logic gates, as illustrated in the partial logic diagram of Figure 2.11. The input of each FF is controlled by an arrangement of four 3-input AND gates and one 4-input OR gate. These logic gates are controlled by four separate control lines, based on the 2-bit input selection lines, S0 and S1. These two binary signals correspond to four control lines, representing the four modes of operation. In one mode, the information in the FFs remains fixed and parallel inputs and outputs are available. In the second operating mode, the data is shifted from left to right. In the third mode, it is shifted from right to left, and in the fourth mode parallel operation of the inputs is enabled.

As illustrated in the logic diagram, the parallel outputs are available at all times.

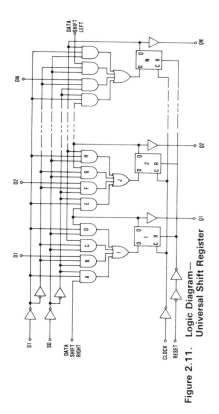

Figure 2.11. Logic Diagram— Universal Shift Register

The clock and reset signal is common to all FFs. In all other respects the universal shift register operates in exactly the same way as the standard shift registers described in Sections 2.9 and 2.10.

KEY PARAMETERS

a) *Power dissipation.* Typical power dissipation is 27 mW for low-power TTL and 425 mW for ECL under no-load conditions.

b) *Quiescent current.* The current drawn by the IC when no operations take place. 5.0 nA is typical at 5 V for low-power CMOS.

c) *Toggle rate.* The maximum clock frequency. 3.6 MHz at 5 V is typical for low-power CMOS, 200 MHz is typical for ECL, and 40 MHz is typical for standard and low-power TTL ICs.

d) *Output rise and fall time.* The time required for the 10% to 90% amplitude of the leading and trailing edge of the output signal. 100 ns is typical for low-power CMOS. 12 ns is typical for low-power TTL, and 2 ns is typical for ECL ICs.

e) *Propagation delay time, clock-to-output.* The time delay from the clock pulse edge until a change in output occurs. 235 ns at 5 V is typical for low-power CMOS, 2.0 ns is typical for ECL, and 20 ns is typical for low-power TTL ICs.

f) *Clock pulse width.* 140 ns is typical for low-power CMOS, 20 ns is typical for low-power TTL, and 2 ns is typical for ECL ICs.

APPLICATIONS

Universal shift registers are used in digital communications and in digital computers. They are used for accumulators in the arithmetic units of central processors of digital computers and other applications where digital data must be shifted in the four possible modes.

COMMENTS

The application of universal shift registers requires timing and other control signals external to the shift register, and for this reason manufacturer's application notes should be carefully consulted.

2.12 BUFFER/INVERTER

DESCRIPTION

The buffer/inverter is one of the key functions used in all digital logic assemblies. As the name implies, this circuit provides a stage of buffering, separation in impedance, between other logic elements and, when it acts as inverter, changes the input signal into its complement. While buffer/inverters are most frequently used in combination with other key logic elements, they are also available as separate ICs, with six individual stages on a single IC, as shown in Figure 2.12.

To illustrate the critical function of the buffer/inverter, Figure 2.12 includes the actual circuit used to implement a buffer/inverter in TTL and CMOS logic. In both circuits the input impedance is higher than the output impedance and the output signal is the inverse, complement, of the input signal.

In the TTL version a buffer/inverter is also available in which R3, Q3 and D2 have been omitted. This allows the user to connect an external collector resistor between the output terminal and Vcc or some other voltage. These "open collector" buffer/inverters are particularly useful for level-shifting applications.

Buffer/inverters are available for every logic family and are combined with other circuits to provide special buffering and inverter functions. Some buffers do not invert the input signal; this is indicated by the omission of the circle at the apex of triangular buffer/inverter symbol.

KEY PARAMETERS

The electrical characteristics are the same as those of the particular IC digital family.

a) *Input load factor.* The number of input loads represented by each buffer/inverter. A typical load factor for TTL and CMOS devices is 1.

b) *Output load factor (fan-out).* The number of output loads of the particular digital IC family that the buffer/inverter can drive. A typical TTL buf-

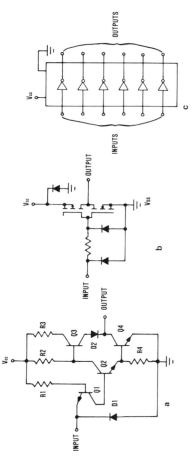

Figure 2.12. (a) TTL Inverter (b) CMOS Inverter (c) Hex Buffer IC

fer/inverter can drive ten TTL inputs. CMOS buffer/inverters can drive a much higher number of CMOS inputs but usually only two TTL loads.

c) *Propagation delay time.* The minimum time a signal is delayed between input and output. For a TTL buffer/inverter 13 ns is typical. For a CMOS device 30 to 80 ns is typical.

d) *Quiescent current.* The current drawn by the entire IC when no operations are performed. For TTL devices 2.0 mA is typical, while 2.0 nA is typical for CMOS

APPLICATIONS

Buffers/inverters are used in all types of digital logic combinations to provide a separation between logic circuits and to increase the fan-out or drive capability of a particular output.

COMMENTS

The description of a hex buffer/inverter indicates that six identical circuits are contained on one IC. Most manufacturers produce the hex buffer ICs for inverting or noninverting applications. Be sure to check the manufacturer's identification number to determine which is which.

2.13 STROBED BUFFER/ INVERTER

DESCRIPTION

This IC provides the basic buffer/inverter function as well as two additional

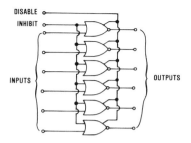

BUFFER/INVERTER

a) STROBED HEX BUFFER BLOCK DIAGRAM

INPUT	INHIB.	DISAB.	OUTPUT
0	0	0	1
1	0	0	0
X	1	0	0
X	X	1	HiZ

X — VALUE IMMATERIAL

b) TRUTH TABLE

Figure 2.13. **(a) Strobed Hex Buffer**
Block Diagram
(b) Truth Table

control functions. As illustrated in Figure
2.13(a), all six inputs are controlled by a
single "inhibit" signal, and all six outputs
are controlled by a single "disable" signal.
This permits each of the six inputs and
outputs to have a total of three possible
states, as indicated by the truth table of
Figure 2.13(b). Because this is an inverting
buffer, when the input is **0** and both the

71

inhibit and disable signals are 0, the output will be 1. When the input is 1, the output will be 0 if both the inhibit and disable signals remain 0. In short, with inhibit and disable signals at 0, the circuit acts as a simple hex inverter/buffer. When the inhibit signal is 1, the output will be 0 regardless of what the input signal will be. If the disable signal is 1, the output will represent a high impedance regardless of what the input of the inhibit signals will be.

KEY PARAMETERS

The electrical characteristics of this IC will be the same as those of the particular digital IC family.

a) *Propagation delay time.* The time delay between input and output of any terminal. 200 ns is typical for CMOS devices.

b) *Minimum disable setup time.* The minimum time it takes from the application from the disable signal until all six buffer/inverters are disabled. 20 to 50 ns is typical for CMOS.

c) *Minimum hold time for disable signal.* The minimum time required for the disable signal to remain on in order for data to be disabled. 25 to 75 ns is typical for CMOS devices.

APPLICATIONS

This IC is useful as a three-state hex inverter for interfacing other ICs with data buses. Other controlled interface applications are also possible.

72

2.14 SCHMITT-TRIGGER BUFFER/INVERTER

DESCRIPTION

This IC, containing six identical circuits, provides the Schmitt-Trigger function and acts as buffer/inverter, as illustrated in the logic diagram of Figure 2.14. It is particularly useful where slowly changing waveforms, such as sinewaves, must be squared up, or where noise immunity must be improved. The Schmitt-Trigger circuit conducts over only a narrow "window," a portion of the total supply voltage. When the input signal is below this hysteresis voltage, nothing passes between input and output. When the input signal reaches the bottom portion of the hysteresis voltage, the Schmitt-Trigger circuit goes into saturation, and when the upper level of the hysteresis voltage is reached, the circuit is cut off. The input signal is changed into a pulse that has the voltage level of the particular logic family. In all other respects the Schmitt-Trigger inverter/buffer functions like all other inverter/buffer circuits.

KEY PARAMETERS

The electrical characteristics are the same as those for the particular digital IC family.

a) *Quiescent current*. The current drawn by the entire IC when no operations are performed. For low-power CMOS

INPUT

SCHMITT TRIGGER

OUTPUT

a) LOGIC DIAGRAM

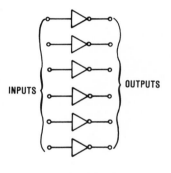

INPUTS

OUTPUTS

b) FUNCTION BLOCK

Figure 2.14. (a) Logic Diagram
(b) Function Block

devices, 0.5 nA and 5 V is typical. For high-voltage CMOS devices, 0.02 mA is typical up to 15 V.

b) *Hysteresis voltage.* The voltage range over which the Schmitt-Trigger fires. 0.55 V is typical for low-power CMOS with a 5 V power supply. For high-voltage CMOS devices 0.9 V is typical for a 5 V power supply.

c) *Threshold voltage.* The actual positive and negative voltage that causes the Schmitt-Trigger circuit to fire and to turn off. For low-power CMOS devices, 2.7 V is a typical positive going and 2.1 V is a typical negative going threshold voltage.

d) *Propagation delay time.* The time required between the arrival of the input signal and the availability of the output signal. For low-power CMOS 125 ns is typical and for high-voltage CMOS devices 140 ns is typical, both at 5 V power supply voltage.

APPLICATIONS

Schmitt-Trigger buffer/inverters are used in wave and pulse shapers, as monostable and as astable multivibrators. They are also used widely as receiving circuits in digital transmission systems because the Schmitt-Trigger action greatly improves noise immunity.

2.15   LINE DRIVERS

DESCRIPTION

The line driver function is available in a variety of IC configurations, and the logic diagram of Figure 2.15(a) illustrates the essential features of one popular configuration. Two sets of four inverting amplifiers are controlled by an enable signal which is passed through a noninverting amplifier. The operation of each individual amplifier is defined by the truth table of Figure 2.15(b). When the enable input is 1, the amplifier output will be a high impedance, regardless of what the input is. Only when the enable input is 0 can the output be the inverse of the input.

As the name implies, this type of circuit is used to transmit digital data over a transmission line of some sort. In most instances this is simply one line on a multi-wire bus connecting digital devices to each other. 660 ohms is the normal impedance used in most digital bus systems, and this should be matched by the output of the line driver when it is enabled. When the driver is not enabled, its output impedance will be much higher. This is important because otherwise the effect of a number of line drivers would load the entire bus system. This type of digital amplifier is frequently called "tristate" because the output of each line driver can be either 1, 0, or high impedance.

KEY PARAMETERS

a) *Power dissipation.* The total power dissipated by the IC during opera-

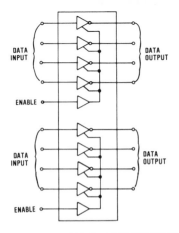

a) LOGIC DIAGRAM — TYPICAL LINE DRIVER IC

ENABLE	INPUT	OUTPUT
1	X	HIGH Z
0	0	1
0	1	0

b) TRUTH TABLE

Figure 2.15. (a) Logic Diagram—Typical
Line Driver IC
(b) Truth Table

77

tion. 325 mW is the typical power dissipation for a standard ECL and 20 mW is typical for low-power TTL.

b) *Quiescent current.* The minimum current through the IC when all amplifiers are in the high impedance state. 100 μ A is typical for TTL and 20μ A is typical for low-power TTL ICs.

c) *Propagation delay time, data input to output.* 100 ns is typical for TTL ICs and 30 ns is typical for low-power TTL types.

d) *Propagation delay time, output disable.* The time required for the enable signal to change the output to a high impedance state. 6 to 10 ns is typical for standard TTL and 25 to 30 ns is typical for low-power TTL.

e) *Output current capability.* The amount of current that each line driver stage can provide. 30 mA is typical for standard TTL and 3 to 6 mA is typical for low-power TTL.

APPLICATIONS

Line drivers are used to amplify digital signals sufficiently so that they can be transmitted over a bus line, coax cable, or some other transmission medium. Most line driver ICs are part of a multi-wire bus system with transmission distances generally less than 50 ft.

COMMENTS

In some literature, line drivers are referred to as tri-state buffers. They differ from the buffer amplifiers described in Section 2.12 because of the three states possible in their output and because they are specifically intended to match the impedance of a digital data bus. Many line drivers are also capable of level shifting to provide compatibility with different IC families.

2.16 LINE RECEIVERS

DESCRIPTION

This IC receives digital signals from a two-wire transmission line, although a multi-wire bus with a common ground can also be received by them. As illustrated in Figure 2.16(a), each amplifier has two inputs, one inverting and one noninverting, and a single output. It is possible to connect one of the two inputs to the reference voltage and thereby set the logic level required for "above noise" reception. Line receivers are generally differential amplifiers with a hysteresis characteristic, similar to or including the Schmitt-Trigger principle.

A balanced input and balanced output line receiver is illustrated in Figure 2.16(b). This type of differential input and differential output amplifier is particularly useful where the amplifier IC acts as a repeater. Note that both of the receiver ICs illustrated in Figure 2.16 are continuously open and not controlled by any gating signal.

KEY PARAMETERS

a) *Power dissipation*. The power required by the entire IC. 100-120 mW is typ-

79

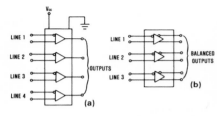

Figure 2.16. (a) Single Output Line
Receiver
(b) Balanced Output Line
Receiver

ical under no-load conditions for ECL
ICs.
b) *Propagation delay time.* The time required from data input to output. 1.5
to 2.0 ns is typical for ECL ICs.

APPLICATIONS

Line receivers are used in the wire transmission portion of digital communications
systems.

2.17 LINE TRANSCEIVERS

DESCRIPTION

In this IC the line driver and receiver
functions are combined in a special two-
stage amplifier network. The logic diagram
of Figure 2.17 shows four line transceivers,
controlled by a single enable gate for the

80

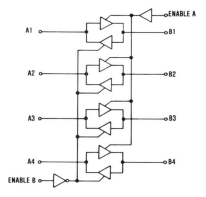

Figure 2.17. Logic Diagram—
Quad Line Transceiver

receive and another enable gate for the
transmitter function. When the enable A
signal is 1 and the enable B signal is 0, the
amplifier going from A1 to B1 will be
operating while the other amplifier going
from B1 to A1 will be in the high output
impedance state. This means that data can
travel from A1 to B1. When enable A is 0
and enable B is 1, the operation is reversed
and data can travel only from B1 to A1. If
all the A terminals are connected to an
exterior bus and all the B terminals to an
interior bus, then the receipt on transmission of information can be completely controlled by changing the logic state of the
enable A and enable B terminals.

While Figure 2.17 shows only four transceivers, ICs are available with as many as

81

eight transceivers, controlled by a single enable gate for transmission and another one for receiving.

KEY PARAMETERS

    a) *Power dissipation.* 100 mW is typical for TTL and 20 mW is typical for low-power TTL ICs.

    b) *Propagation delay time.* The time from data input to output. 12 ns is typical for low-power TTL ICs.

    c) *Propagation delay time, enable to output.* The time from the enable pulse until an output appears. 20 ns is typical for low-power TTL ICs.

APPLICATIONS

Line transceivers are widely used in the input/output (I/O) sections of digital computers and their peripherals.

COMMENTS

Line transceivers are sometimes found as part of a complete I/O computer section. The key feature is that both directional amplifiers are of the tri-state kind.

2.18 COUNTERS/DIVIDERS

DESCRIPTION

The essential function in all counters/ dividers is performed by the basic flip-flop

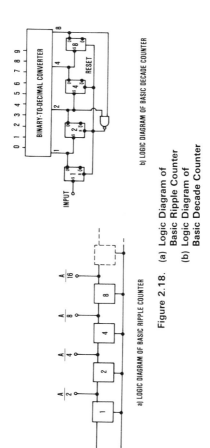

a) LOGIC DIAGRAM OF BASIC RIPPLE COUNTER

b) LOGIC DIAGRAM OF BASIC DECADE COUNTER

Figure 2.18. (a) Logic Diagram of
Basic Ripple Counter
(b) Logic Diagram of
Basic Decade Counter

83

(FF) which changes state only on either a positive or a negative going transaction. If a pulse or square-wave signal is applied to the input of an FF with positive logic, it will change state only on the rising edge of the signal. For every two pulses or square waves at the input, only one square wave will be available at the output. Every FF has a Q and a $\overline{Q}$ output, one being the complement of the other. A detailed discussion of FFs is presented in Section 2.5.

The term *counter* implies that pulses or square waves are counted, and this function is provided by adding logic gates to the basic FF configuration. The term *divider* more accurately describes the function of the FFs themselves since each FF stage divides the input frequency by two. In some applications the input frequency is divided by the series of FFs into another frequency that is a predetermined fraction of the input. In other applications the pulses applied to the input are counted and a logic output signal is generated when a previously specified number of pulses has passed through the counter. Because both counting and division can be performed by all devices described in this section, we will, from now on, use only the term *counter*.

A basic "ripple" counter is illustrated in the logic diagram of Figure 2.18(a). A square-wave signal is supplied at input A and A/2 appears at the Q output terminal of FF1. As illustrated, each stage divides its input frequency by two. The FFs are numbered according to the binary system. Note that FF1 operates at half of the input of the frequency, while FF8 will operate at 1/16 of the input frequency. If the output of the fourth stage (FF8) were connected to the reset line, this counter would count only the first 16 pulses. Once the 16th pulse has set FF8, the reset signal will prevent any further counting.

The logic diagram of 2.18(b) illustrates the minimum circuitry for a decade counter. Here, the NAND circuit senses the Q signal from FF2 and the Q signal from FF8. When both occur at the same time, the counter has counted a total of ten pulses of square waves, and the reset line is activated. The four Q outputs will then represent the binary equivalent of the decimal number ten. During the first nine pulses which appear at the input, the binary equivalents of the corresponding decimal numbers will appear at the Q outputs, and these are converted to the decimal numbers 0 through 9.

Almost all of the counters described in this section are available with either straight binary or binary-coded decimal (BCD) outputs. Counters are also available in two main categories, depending on the manner of operation. The basic ripple counter shown in Figure 2.18 is considered asynchronous because it operates independently of a clock. It could be connected to a photocell which counts people passing through a gate. In this application it would count asynchronous events. In many digital logic applications, however, the counter operates under the control of a clock signal. This greatly reduces the chances of triggering by noise or other unwanted signals, but it also requires that the input signal be synchronized with the clock signal. In many synchronous counters the input and the clock are the same signal. Special features, such as programmable division by any number or up and down counting, are available in both synchronous and asynchronous, binary and BCD counters. A wide variety of counters and special features is available in each of the different digital IC families.

KEY PARAMETERS

The electrical characteristics are essentially those of the particular digital IC family.

a) *Maximum operating frequency.* This is the highest input frequency that a ripple (asynchronous) counter can accept. For synchronous counters this also determines the highest clock frequency. The maximum operating frequency depends, to some extent, on the digital IC family used. TTL counters have a higher operating frequency than CMOS types.

b) *Minimum input signal rise time.* Unless a Schmitt-Trigger circuit is used in the input, slowly changing signals will not activate the counter. Sine waves and varying DC voltages are acceptable only when a Schmitt-Trigger input is used.

c) *Cascading.* When several counter ICs are used in cascade, a carry-out signal from the last stage must be available as input for the next counter IC.

d) *Input polarity.* Indicates whether the FFs in the counter will change on positive (rising) or negative (falling) edges.

e) *Available connections.* On some counters the Q terminal of each FF is available, and in others some of the FF input circuits are also available. This permits the user to connect stages of the counter for a variety of applications. In some counters decoding circuitry is included, and only the fully decoded outputs are available.

f) *Noise characteristics.* Indicate the relation of logic levels to noise signals. To some extent, this characteristic is dependent on the particular digital IC family.

g) *Output load.* In some counters, output driver circuits are included, while in others only a minimum output load can be connected. To some extent, output load capability depends on the particular digital IC family.

h) *Propagation delay.* Normally stated as the time required from the input to the first Q terminal output. Total delays for the entire counter must be calculated, considering the number of stages and the frequency division performed. The basic propagation delay time depends on the particular digital IC family.

i) *Control signal delay.* The time required from the application of a particular control signal, such as reset, preset, up/down, until the control signal takes effect.

APPLICATIONS

Counters are used for frequency division, as control timers, to drive time displays, as part of phase-locked loops, and in a host of other applications where either time or a number of events are being counted.

COMMENTS

The various types of counters described in the following pages do not exhaust the full gamut of available counters. Special purpose counters, such as those used for digital clock radios, for color TV circuitry and other special applications, are also available.

2.19 COUNTER, SYNCHRONOUS

DESCRIPTION

Synchronous counters are available in a large variety of sizes and with a number of standard output decoders. The essential features of this type of counter can be seen from the illustration of Figure 2.19(a). Each of the flip-flops (FF) is controlled by the clock signal. Whatever data are entered must be entered in synchronism with the clock, because only when the clock enables each FF can the counting or dividing operation take place. As indicated in the waveform diagram of Figure 2.19(b), all the output signals, Q1 through Q4, have the same symmetrical pulse shape. If we assume that the data input is the same as the clock signal, each output pulse will be the width of one complete square-wave cycle of the clock. Note that each output occurs one

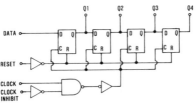

(a) Logic Diagram of Synchronous Counter

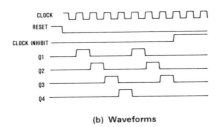

(b) Waveforms

Figure 2.19. (a) Logic Diagram of
Synchronous
Counter
(b) Waveforms

complete clock cycle after the previous one.
The reset signal can be enabled at any time
and, in the illustration of Figure 2.19(b), it is
kept at logic 0 after the start. The clock
inhibit signal, however, has been set to
logic 1 after seven clock cycles and all
output signals remain at 0 thereafter. As

indicated, the counter is advanced one count during each positive signal transaction, as long as the clock inhibit signal is at **0**.

KEY PARAMETERS

The electrical characteristics are essentially the same as those of a particular digital IC family.

a) *Maximum clock input frequency.* Up to about 5.5 MHz for CMOS and 35 MHz for TTL devices.

b) *Clock pulse width.* The maximum width of the clock input signal. This ranges from 60 to 200 ns for CMOS ICs and as low as 20 ns for TTL devices.

c) *Reset pulse width.* The minimum width of the reset pulse. CMOS devices range from 60 to 300 ns, while TTL devices reset pulse widths are approximately 20 ns.

d) *Reset removal time.* The minimum time required until the reset signal is removed and the counter operation is again enabled. A typical value for CMOS devices is 150 to 400 ns.

e) *Maximum power dissipation.* In some instances stated for the total package, in others per output stage. For CMOS a typical value is 500 mW from −40 to +60° C. TTL ICs are available with power dissipations of 100 mW for up to six output stages.

APPLICATIONS

Synchronous counters are used in decade and binary computer control and timing circuits, for decade counters in clock displays, divide-by-N counting, and for frequency division.

COMMENTS

Most commercially available synchronous counters include additional gating and decoding circuits, making their logic diagram more complex than that presented in Figure 2.19.

2.20 COUNTER, ASYNCHRONOUS (RIPPLE)

DESCRIPTION

This type of counter can accept data which occur at any time. Whenever a new transition appears at the input, the effect of this change ripples down through the series of flip-flops (FF). Because there is no clock input to control the transition of each FF, an asynchronous counter is more subject to random noise than a synchronous counter. The logic diagram of Figure 2.20(a) illustrates the simplicity of a straight binary asynchronous counter. Only the data and reset inputs and an output from each FF are required. Assuming that the data is a square wave, as illustrated in the waveform diagram of 2.20(b), and the reset line is at logic **0**, the output of the four stages will "ripple" through, as illustrated. Note that the frequency of Q1 is half of the frequency

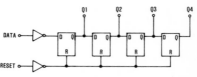

(a) Logic Diagram of Asynchronous Counter

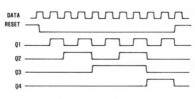

(b) Waveforms

Figure 2.20. (a) Logic Diagram of
Asynchronous
Counter
(b) Waveforms

of the data input, Q2 is half of the frequency
of Q1, Q3 half the frequency of Q2, etc.
Because of the inverter connected to the
data input, the first FF appears to trigger
on the negative going edge. When the reset
signal changes from logic 0 to logic 1, all of
the outputs are reset to 0.

KEY PARAMETERS

The electrical characteristics are essentially those of the particular digital IC
family.

a) *Quiescent current.* Total current drawn when counter is not operating. 5.0 nA is typical at 5 V for CMOS ICs.

b) *Maximum input frequency.* 8 MHz is typical for CMOS, and up to 50 MHz is possible with TTL ICs.

c) *Input transition time.* Very short rise and fall times of the input signal are limited by the maximum input signal frequency. Very long rise and fall times can be accommodated in those devices which have Schmitt-Trigger or similar hysteresis type input circuits. Many CMOS devices have no stated limits for this parameter.

d) *Reset pulse width.* Minimum values for CMOS devices range from 250 to 500 ns. For TTL devices this will range from 50 to 100 ns.

e) *Reset removal time.* The time required after the reset has gone to logic **0** until the counter is operational again. For CMOS ICs, 150 to 250 ns is typical, while 20 to 100 ns is usually specified for TTL ICs.

APPLICATIONS

Asynchronous counters are used for event counting, pulse counting in radio isotope detection applications, timing control, and similar applications. They are particularly useful in applications where the events to be counted or measured occur at random or pseudo-random intervals.

COMMENTS

Most asynchronous counters are supplied with additional control and output logic circuits, making them more complex than indicated in the logic of Figure 2.20. Some manufacturers list them as ripple counters, while others classify them as asynchronous.

2.21   COUNTER, UP/DOWN

DESCRIPTION

The key feature of this IC is the ability of an otherwise ordinary counter to count either down or up. This makes it possible to enter a number of pulses during one period and then to subtract a second number from the first by counting down that number of pulses. While many up/down counters are programmable or presettable, the function block illustrated in Figure 2.21 omits this feature and shows only the controls necessary for the up and down counting operation and cascading. When the counter is full, the carry-out terminal is used to feed the overflow into the next cascaded IC. The CF terminal serves as input of either the original signal or the overflow from a previous cascaded section. A master reset, a clock inhibit and a clock input are provided, but the key feature is the up/down mode control. When this terminal is at 1, the counter operates in a normal counting-up mode. When the up/down mode control is 0, the counter will count down.

KEY PARAMETERS

The electrical characteristics will be the same as for the particular digital IC family.

a) *Up/down setup time.* The time required to change counter operation from up to down or back to up. Typical values for low-power CMOS range from 50 to 170 ns. For TTL devices, 20 to 30 ns is typical.

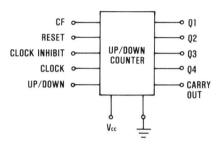

Figure 2.21

APPLICATIONS

Whenever up/down counting capability is required. Widely used in difference counting and frequency synthesizer applications. This IC also found in A/D and D/A converter systems and in computers to generate magnitudes and polarity signs.

COMMENTS

Up/down counters are available with programmable inputs, with divide-by-N features, and with other capabilities.

2.22 DECODERS/ENCODERS

DESCRIPTION

Decoders are essentially an arrangement of logic elements which are combined to change from one digital code to another. The term "decoder" is most frequently used but, depending on the point of view, the term "encoder" is equally correct.

Figure 2.22 shows the logic diagram of a 3-bit binary-to-1-of-8 decoder. The inputs A, B and C can represent any logic function, and the outputs 1 through 8 will then provide the addition or the logic OR function of these three inputs. In order to produce the complement of the input fractions, the OR circuits have inverters at the inputs indicated by the small circle. As an example, output 4 is $A + B + C$. If the input A, B and C were each logic **1**s, output 4 would be **1**. If $A = 0$, $\overline{B} = 1$, $\overline{C} = 1$, then output 4 is **0**. A close look at the logic diagram of Figure 2.22 shows that it represents the conversion from a 3-bit binary to an octal number. Output 1 represents the octal number 7 and output 8 represents the octal number 0.

The most widely used types of decoders are presented in the following pages. In addition to these standard ICs, special purpose decoders are found in some digital logic systems. Decoders are available in all of the commonly used digital IC families, such as CMOS, TTL, ECL, etc.

KEY PARAMETERS

The electrical characteristics are essentially the same as those of the particular digital IC family.

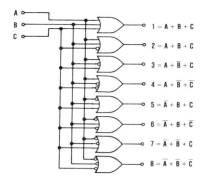

LOGIC DIAGRAM OF 3-BIT BINARY TO 1-OF-8 DECODER

Figure 2.22. Logic Diagram of 3-Bit Binary to 1-of-8 Decoder

a) *Maximum power dissipation.* The maximum power dissipated by the IC when in operation. This will vary according to the digital IC family and also according to the number of stages or logic elements used.

b) *Quiescent current.* The current used by the entire IC when no operations take place. This will vary according to the digital IC family and according to the number of logic elements used.

c) *Noise immunity.* The relation of the noise amplitude as a percentage of the power supply voltage. This parameter usually depends on the digital IC family.

d) *Propagation delay time.* The time required from input to output. While this depends, to some extent, on the digital IC family, the complexity of the logic gating and the number of stages between input and output are also important factors.

e) *Control signals.* Some decoders have means of enabling all or part of the inputs or outputs. Special input and output terminals to permit cascading decoders are also available in some decoders.

APPLICATIONS

Decoders are used in digital systems whenever it is necessary to change from one code to another. Specific applications are presented for the different decoders described in the following pages.

2.23 DECODER, BCD-TO-DECIMAL

DESCRIPTION

This type of decoder is probably the most widely used in all digital systems because it changes the inherent binary codes used within the system to the decimal code used by the human operators. Figure 2.23 illustrates the function block of a basic BCD-to-decimal decoder. Four input lines, representing the four BCD values, result in ten output lines, representing the decimal num-

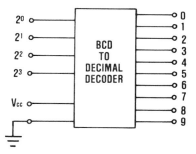

Figure 2.23.

bers 0 through 9. This type of decoder is often used in combination with decade counters and with decimal displays. By using only the three least significant inputs, a 3-bit binary-to-octal decoder is obtained, with outputs only on terminal 0 through 7.

KEY PARAMETERS

The electrical characteristics are essentially the same as those of the particular digital IC family.

a) *Quiescent current.* The total current flowing in the IC when no operations are performed. 5.0 nA at 5 V power supply is typical for low-power CMOS.

b) *Noise immunity.* The relation of noise amplitude to V_{cc}. 45% of the power-

99

supply voltage is typical for low-power CMOS.

c) *Propagation delay time.* The time required from the input to the output of the IC. Typical values are 300 ns at 5 V power supply for low-power CMOS devices.

APPLICATIONS

BDC-to-decimal decoders are used for code conversion, address decoding, memory selection control, read-out decoding, and demultiplexing in digital systems such as mini- and microcomputers, digital volt-meters, etc.

2.24 DISPLAY DRIVER, BCD-TO-7-SEGMENT

DESCRIPTION

The universal use of 7-segment numerical displays has resulted in a wide range of ICs capable of driving them. One of the most widely used is illustrated in the block diagram of Figure 2.24. The BCD input is applied to a set of four flip-flops which are used as a "latch." The "strobe" signal determines when the information presented at the input is stored in the latch and when it is erased. The BCD-to-7-segment decoder has seven separate driver stages.

As illustrated in Figure 2.24, a lamp test and a blanking signal are applied to the decoder portion. The purpose of the lamp test signal is to illuminate all seven sections of the numerical display, and the blanking signal can be used to turn off the entire display for zero blanking multi-digit displays, or else to control the on-off time when a series of displays operates in a power conserving, multiplexed mode.

The voltage and current capability of the driver stage determine which type of 7-segment numerical displays can be driven. A typical high-voltage CMOS IC can operate up to a maximum of 20 V and can source up to 25 mA at each output. This makes it possible to drive LED displays, low-voltage fluorescent displays, and even incandescent displays. To drive liquid crystal displays (LCDs), some other characteristics are necessary.

KEY PARAMETERS

The electrical characteristics are essentially those of the particular IC family.

a) *Maximum power dissipation.* 500 mW for a high-voltage CMOS IC. 250 mW for TTL ICs.

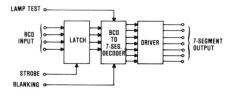

Figure 2.24. Block Diagram—BCD-to-7-Segment LED Driver

b) *Quiescent current.* The maximum current drawn when the IC is not operating. 100 mA at 20 V supply and +25°C is typical for high-voltage CMOS.

c) *Propagation delay time.* The time required between data input and output. A maximum of 1,000 ns is typical for high-voltage CMOS devices at 5 V power supply.

d) *Minimum setup time.* The minimum time required from the data input until it is stored in the latches. 150 ns is typical for high-voltage CMOS ICs.

e) *Strobe pulse width.* The minimum width of the strobe signal controlling the storage of the data. 400 ns for high-voltage CMOS at 5 V supply.

f) *Output circuit.* The method of driving the different types of displays determines what type of output circuit should be used. Many high-voltage CMOS devices use an open-collector-emitter circuit, and this requires separate series resistors for each output when driving an LED. Low-voltage fluorescent displays can be driven directly, but incandescent displays require a small pull-up resistor for each output to the power-supply voltage.

APPLICATIONS

This IC is used to drive common-cathode LED displays either as single units, or as multiplexed series of displays. Incandescent and low-voltage fluorescent displays can also be driven with this IC.

2.25 ARITHMETIC FUNCTIONS

DESCRIPTION

This section deals with digital ICs that perform the basic arithmetic functions, using the binary system. Human beings are accustomed to the decimal system, but digital logic is based on the binary system, which recognizes only two values, *0* and *1*. The position of each *0* or *1* in a series determines its value, just as we have tens, hundreds, thousands, etc., in the decimal system. The least significant bit in the binary system is $2°$, which can be either *0* or *1*. The next significant bit has the value of 2^1 (*0* or *2*) and after that, the powers of 2 increase (2^2, 2^3, etc.). The decimal number 9 is represented by 1001, which adds 2^3 (8) to the least significant bit, 2^0 (1).

The following fundamentals of binary arithmetic apply to all of the arithmetic functions described in this section. Figure 2.25 illustrates how the addition and subtraction functions are implemented in digital logic. The half adder consists of an exclusive OR and an AND circuit. As illustrated by the truth table, the rules for addition are carefully followed. The full adder is comprised of two half adders and an OR circuit for the carry-out. The truth table illustrates the operation of full addition of two binary values, A and B.

A	B	SUM	CARRY
0	0	0	0
0	1	1	0
1	0	1	0
1	1	0	1

(a) Half Adder

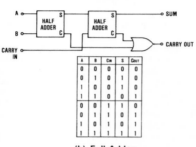

A	B	C_{IN}	S	C_{OUT}
0	0	0	0	0
0	1	0	1	0
1	0	0	1	0
1	1	0	0	1
0	0	1	1	0
0	1	1	0	1
1	0	1	0	1
1	1	1	1	1

(b) Full Adder

Figure 2.25. (a) Half Adder
              (b) Full Adder

1) *Rules for addition;* $0 + 0 = 0$;
   $1 + 0 = 1$; $1 + 1 = 0$ (carry 1).

Examples:

$$\begin{array}{rr} 101 & 5 \\ + 001 & + 1 \\ \hline 110 & 6 \end{array} \qquad \begin{array}{rr} 111 & 7 \\ + 011 & + 3 \\ \hline 1010 & 10 \end{array}$$

      carry   carry

2) *Rules for subtraction:* $0 - 0 = 0$;
   $1 - 0 = 1$; $0 - 1 = 1$ (borrow 1);
   $1 - 1 = 0$.

Examples:

```
    0 borrow
      110     6  (minuend)
    − 001   − 1  (subtrahend)
      101     5
```

```
   01 ← borrow
      1001    9  (minuend)
    − 0011  − 3  (subtrahend)
      0110    6
```

An alternate method of binary subtraction involves either the *1's* complement or the *2's* complement. In *1's* complement all *0* and *1* in the subtrahend are interchanged and this complemented number is then added to the minuend. The last *1* carry is added as least significant bit to the total sum.

1's complement example:

```
      5      101      101  (minuend)
    − 3    − 011    + 100  (subtrahend)
      2             ⌐1001
                    ⌐+   1
                      010
```

In the *2's* complement method of subtrahend is complemented by changing *0* into *1* and *1* into *0* in the same way, but an extra *1* is added to the subtrahend before it is added to the minuend. The last carry is omitted.

2's complement example:

```
      5      101                    101
    − 3    − 011 → 100 + 1 =      + 101
      2                    drop 1 _____
                                    010
```

3) *Rules for multiplication:* $1 \times 1 = 1$;
   $1 \times 0 = 0$.

Examples:

```
  101   5 × 3          100   4 × 5
× 011               × 101
  101                 100
  101                 000
 1111   15            100
                    10100   20
```

In many arithmetic operations multiplication is performed by repeated addition.

4) *Rules for division:* $1/1 = 1$; $0/1 = 0$;

Examples:

```
   101      5           101      5
11)1111   3)15    100)10100   4)20
   11                   100
     11                 100
     11                 100
     00                 000
```

In many arithmetic operations division is performed by repeated subtraction, and the result is given by the number of times the subtraction can be carried out.

2.26   4-BIT FULL ADDER

DESCRIPTION

This IC accepts two 4-bit binary numbers and adds them in a parallel operation. As illustrated in Figure 2.26, one set of binary numbers is connected to inputs A1 through A4, and the second number is connected to inputs B1 and B4. Carry information from previous arithmetic operations can be connected to the C_{IN} terminal.

Four standard full adders are used, with a carry signal progressing from adder 1 through adder 4. At the same time, special high-speed parallel carry operation is available for use with other adders in a large arithmetic system.

The truth table of Figure 2.26 describes the operation of any one of the full adders. A carry output occurs only when both A and B are in the logic 1 state. The lower half of the truth table illustrates the operation when there is a carry-in. (See page 108)

KEY PARAMETERS

The electrical characteristics are those of the particular digital IC family.

a) *Operating speed.* 160 ns is the typical time required from the input of the two binary numbers to the output of the sum and the carry. (These values are typical for low-power CMOS devices.)

b) *Quiescent current.* The total current required by the IC when no operations are performed. 5.0 nA at 5 V is typical for low-power CMOS devices.

c) *Output load.* Each output of this IC can drive two low-power TTL loads. (Typical for low-power CMOS.)

APPLICATIONS

This IC is used in the arithmetic logic unit (ALU) of some computers to perform basic arithmetic functions.

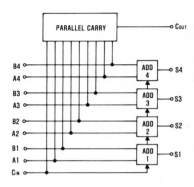

(a) Block Diagram

Cᵢₙ	B	A	C_OUT	S
0	0	0	0	0
0	0	1	0	1
0	1	0	0	1
0	1	1	1	0
1	0	0	0	1
1	0	1	1	0
1	1	0	1	0
1	1	1	1	1

(b) Truth Table (One Stage)

Figure 2.26. (a) Block Diagram
              (b) Truth Table (One Stage)

Chapter 3

Chapter Three deals with all types of memory ICs. Beginning with the fundamental memory concepts, we include dynamic RAM, static RAM and the basic FIFO memories. Serial shift registers are also included because of their essential applications as memories.

Chapter Three also contains the different types of read-only-memory (ROM) that are available on ICs. This includes the PROM, the EAROM and the EPROM.

The reader will understand that a particular type of memory IC will have the same organization and functions, regardless of the number of bits or bytes that it can store.

3.1 MEMORY

This chapter presents the functional operation of the various memory ICs on the market. Detailed technical information pertaining to the IC's construction, such as NMOS, MOS, TTL, as well as exact timing characteristics, etc., is not presented here but is available in the manufacturer's data.

Memory ICs store binary bits which represent data. Instructions of a control program used in computer systems, data values, parameters, etc., are a few examples. This binary information is generally formatted as a group of binary bits, defined as a word.

The operation of the memory IC can be understood from Figure 3.1. When the memory array is updated with new data words, a write signal is generated. This causes the data word on the data bus-in lines to be stored in the memory array. The location in the array is determined by the binary value on the address bus. If the data stored in the memory array is to be accessed, a read signal is activated. This transfers the stored data to the data-out lines. The detailed operation varies from memory IC to IC. Some ICs have only a read operation because the binary bit patterns are always

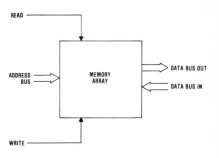

Figure 3.1.   Basic Memory Functions

stored in the IC. Other ICs do not have the input address bus.

Data Access: There are two basic types of memory ICs by this classification:

a) *Random Access.* The memory array is constructed as a block of words with each word consisting of "n" number of bits. Access to any word in the memory array is random. Address decode logic (ADL) is included in the IC to perform this function and the inputs to the ADL are connected to the address bus. The binary value on the address bus is decoded for the ADL, causing the activation of the word select line. Each select line is connected to one of the words in the memory array. A read or write operation will result in a data transfer in or out of the memory IC.

b) *Serial Access.* The memory array is constructed to store blocks of data bits in series. There is only one input and one output data line and no address decode logic is required. (The exception to this is the charge coupled device (CCD) where the address decode logic is used to access the blocks of data.) If the data block is to be read out of the IC, all of the data must first be moved until the desired block is positioned at the output of the IC. Once positioned, the data transfer takes place.

Non-Volatile vs. Volatile Memory ICs: Within each group of memory ICs a further classification can be distinguished:

a) *Volatile Memory.* The binary data stored in the memory array is lost when power is removed from the IC. Upon reapplying power to the IC, the data must be rewritten into the memory array. As a general rule, higher speeds of operation can be used for the read/write cycles.

b) *Non-Volatile Memory.* The binary data stored in the memory array is retained when power is removed from the IC. Upon reapplying power to the IC, the data is preserved and can be instantaneously utilized. As a general rule the speed of the write cycle is slow and that of the read cycle is fast.

3.2 DYNAMIC RANDOM-ACCESS MEMORY (RAM)

DESCRIPTION

The dynamic RAM IC stores binary data words. The design of dynamic RAM allows the user to access any memory location by setting the address inputs to the selected binary value. Once selected, data is written into or read from the memory cells. The dynamic RAM is volatile. Removal of power results in the loss of data in the memory array. Figure 3.2 illustrates the operation of the dynamic RAM.

"Refresh" Mode: Higher bit density, lower power dissipation, and faster read/write operations are achieved with capacitive type of memory cells, but these capacitors must be recharged or "refreshed" periodically to retain the data in the memory array. Internal or external clock generators with suitable control logic must be provided for reliable "refresh" operation.

Write Operation: The address bus to the dynamic RAM IC is decoded by the column and row address decode logic. The outputs select a specific memory location. When the chip select and write command is activated, the data value at the data inputs is written into the selected memory location.

Read Operation: The read operation is similar to the write operation except that a read rather than a write command is generated. This results in routing the contents of the selected memory location through the data I/O circuits to the data output bus.

KEY PARAMETERS

a) *Read cycle time.* The time required from the leading edge of the read command until the contents of the selected memory are available at the output of the data I/O buffers. Typical values are 300 to 600 ns.

b) *Write cycle time.* The time required from the leading edge of the write command until the data bit(s) at the data I/O buffer are written into the selected memory location. Typical values are 300 to 600 ns.

c) *Access time.* The time between the application of the column and row address bit control signals and the start of the read or write signals. Typical values are 100 to 300 ns.

d) *Refresh time.* The maximum time allowed to activate all row address lines in order to retain the data stored

113

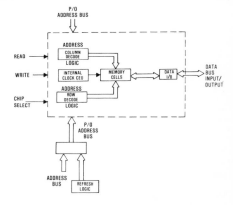

Figure 3.2. Dynamic RAM

in the memory cell(s). Typical maximum time is 2 ms.

e) *Power supply*. The voltage(s) required to operate the dynamic RAM as a memory element. Typical voltages for MOS dynamic RAMs are −5 V, +5 V, +12 V.

f) *Power dissipation*. This value, in milliwatts, is the product of the supply voltage and the current consumption by the IC.

Operating: The power dissipation of the IC when the IC is being operated as a memory element. Typical values are 300 to 600 mW.

Standby: The power dissipation of the IC when the IC is not active but the data stored

in the memory cell(s) is
retained. The ranges of
values are 50 to 40 mW.

g) *Memory organization.* The structure
of the memory IC depending on the
number of words and the number of
binary bits for each word. Typical
sizes are 1024 words by 1, 2 and 4 bits
to 16,384 words by 1 bit.

APPLICATIONS

The dynamic RAM IC is used where
large amounts of changing binary data bits
are to be stored, as in computers, data processors, word generators, etc.

COMMENTS

Because of their design, dynamic RAM
memory systems require more logic elements than do static RAMs due to the
"refresh" requirements for the memory
cells. Care must be taken to insure that the
refresh timing function does not interfere
with the normal read/write function. The
various input/output lines to the dynamic
RAM may operate at different interface
voltage levels.

3.3 STATIC RANDOM-ACCESS MEMORY (RAM)

DESCRIPTION

The static RAM IC allows random selection of any memory location in the mem-

ory array. Static RAMs are volatile and allow the storage of the data in the memory array without the need of clocks or "refresh" logic (see Dynamic RAM). Static RAM operation is described below and illustrated in Figure 3.3.

Write Operation: Data to be stored in the memory array are connected to the data input/output lines of the RAM IC. The location at which data will be stored is determined by the encoded word at the address inputs to the RAM. This value is decoded by the address decoder logic. The result is the activation of one of the memory select lines connected to the desired location in the memory array. The chip select line is activated, connecting the data input lines to the memory array, and the input control logic is enabled. The write command is then generated, causing the contents of the selected memory location to be updated to the new data word.

Read Operation: The selected memory location is determined by the decoding of the binary input by the address decode logic. This activates the selected memory location. When the chip enable line is activated and the read command is generated, the contents of the selected memory location are connected to the data output lines.

KEY PARAMETERS

a) *Read cycle time.* The time required from the leading edge of the read command until the contents of the selected memory location are trans-

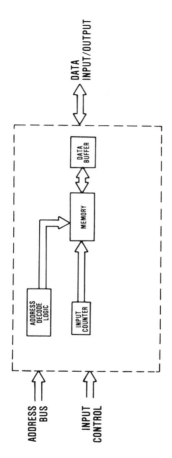

Figure 3.3. Static RAM

ferred to the output of the data I/O buffers. Typical values are 40 nanoseconds to 450 ns.

b) *Write cycle time.* The time required from the leading edge of the write command until the binary data at the data I/O buffer are written (stored) into the memory cells. Typical values range from 35 to 500 ns.

c) *Access time.* The time required from the beginning of the chip select and the address signals to the start of the read/write commands. Typical values are 10 to 100 ns.

d) *Power supply.* The voltages required to operate the static RAM as a memory element. Typically, a single voltage is used at +5 V.

e) *Power dissipation.* The product of the current consumed by the IC and the specified voltage. Due to the wide variety of memory sizes available, this range of values is expressed on a per-bit basis. The power dissipation (PD) can vary from .04 mW/Bit to .15 mW/Bit. To determine the total power dissipation use the formula: total power dissipation = (number of words) × the (bits per word) × (PD per bit). Note: Those static RAMs designed with MOS technology have a standby mode which significantly reduces the power dissipation when the memory is not accessed.

f) *Memory organization.* The structure of the RAM IC is expressed as the number of words and the numbers of bits per word. Memory sizes range from 16 words by 4 bits to 16,384 words by 1 bit.

APPLICATIONS

Used to store changing binary data in equipment which requires high-speed operation such as cache memories, computer main frame memory, buffer storage, etc.

3.4 FIRST-IN/FIRST-OUT MEMORY (FIFO)

DESCRIPTION

The FIFO consists of serial memory which stores binary data. The data can be written into the IC at one frequency, while simultaneously data is read from the memory at a different frequency. Control logic within the FIFO IC keeps track of the data once it is stored in the serial memory. This includes processing the data and setting status indicators when the FIFO is empty or full. Most FIFO memories are volatile.

Write Operation: Data on the inputs of the FIFO can be written into the serial memory when the input ready line is activated. Data is transferred into the serial memory when the input ready signal is enabled and the shift input pulse is generated. The internal control logic will shift the data towards the output of the serial memory. Shifting will continue until the data word is in the memory location adjacent to the previously stored data word. The data, once written into the FIFO, cannot be read until all previously stored data words are shifted out.

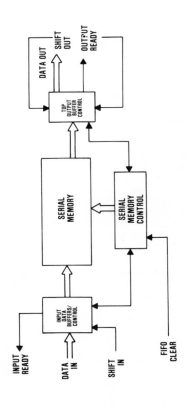

Figure 3.4. FIFO

Read Operation: If data is stored in the FIFO, the output ready line will be activated. If the FIFO was empty, the output ready signal line will be deactivated. Generation of a shift output pulse when the output ready is enabled will result in the transfer of the data from the FIFO through the data out buffer. It is a destructive read since the data is shifted by one location. The activation of the clear input to the FIFO results in erasure of all data in the FIFO.

KEY PARAMETERS

a) *Shift-in frequency.* The speed at which the data entering the FIFO can be transferred into the main memory for automatic processing. (Typical ranges are DC to 15 MHz.b)

b) *Input ready.* The input ready signal indicates that data can be transferred to the serial memory. It is deactivated 50 ns after a shift input pulse is generated. When the input ready signal is disabled, the serial memory is full.

c) *Shift-out pulse frequency.* The frequency at which data can be transferred from the main memory to the output buffers. DC to 15 MHz.

d) *Output ready.* The output ready signal is activated whenever data is available in the serial memory. When the serial memory is empty the output ready signal is disabled.

e) *Latency time.* The time it takes to shift the binary data through the serial memory to the output buffer. This can vary from 2 to 6 ns.

f) *Master FIFO clear.* The FIFO clear, when activated, clears all the FIFO memory cells out. Typical time required is 30 ns to 2 ms.

g) *FIFO organization.* The organization of the FIFO is based on the number of bits per word. Typical structures are 64 words of 9 bits each. Note: The FIFOs are designed for expansion to any number of words and any number of bits.

APPLICATIONS

FIFOs are often used between two systems which operate at two different frequencies. For example, the input buffers are connected to a disc controller operating at 4 MHz while the output buffers are connected to main memory operating at 2 MHz.

COMMENTS

Expansion of the number of words in a FIFO system is achieved by connecting the data output buffers of one FIFO IC to the data input buffers of another FIFO. The output ready and shift-out of the first FIFO IC is connected to the shift-in and input ready lines of the next FIFO.

Expansion of the number of bits per word is achieved by connecting all the shift lines and input ready lines together. This is also done for the shift output ready lines. Access to the binary data stored in the serial memory is not available to the user until it ripples through the serial memory and all previous data is shifted out.

3.5   SERIAL SHIFT REGISTERS

DESCRIPTION

In this type of memory the data is stored in serial form. Access to selected binary bits is accomplished by generating the appropriate number of shift pulses until the bit is at the output line. Shift register memories are volatile. Refer to Chapter 2 for details on shift registers. The typical block diagram for shift registers (SR) is illustrated in Figure 3.5.

Write Operation: The binary word to be stored in the shift register is connected to its data inputs. The recirculate line must be deactivated in order to allow new data to be stored in the SR. After the data word is stabilized, the shift pulse results in the transfer of the data word into the memory cells of the SR. This cycle is repeated for each data word. At the output of the SR the data is transferred to its data out lines.

Read Operation: Since the SR is used as a serial memory IC, data is shifted through the register until it reaches the last set of memory cells where it is connected to the data out lines. In order to prevent losing data, the recirculate line connects the output of the SR last set of cells back to its inputs. Shift pulses cause the output data to be shifted to the input memory cells. New data cannot be transferred into the SR during the recirculate mode.

External logic keeps track of the data block stored in the SR. Bit tracking counters

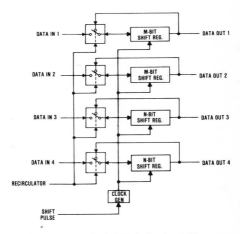

Figure 3.5. Serial Shift Register Memory

are used as indicators to where the start of
the data block is inside the register. In
addition, a word length counter is used,
indicating the length of the data block.

KEY PARAMETERS

a) *Shift pulse frequency.* The range of
pulse repetition frequencies at which
the shift pulses shift the data through
the register. The frequency range is
up to 4 MHz for static SRs.

b) *Set-up time.* The time required for the
data to be at the input to the SR prior
to the generation of shift pulse. Minimum set-up time is 60 ns.

124

c) *Data hold.* The time the data must hold at the input to the shift registers while the shift pulse is generated. Minimum time is 60 ns.

d) *Shift register (memory) organization.* As in RAMs, the SR IC is organized by the number of words and the number of bits per words. Typical organizational structures range from 64 words by 8 bits to 1024 words by 1 bit.

e) *Shift register technology.* Two types of serial shift registers are available—static and dynamic.

Dynamic SR: This type of shift register requires a shift pulse to be generated at least once every 2 ms ("refresh" rate) to prevent the data from being lost. The design of the dynamic shift register is more complex than the static registers. Due to the "refresh" logic required, the trade-off is higher bit density, lower power dissipation, and faster operation.

Static SR: There is no requirement to refresh the static shift register. This simplifies the design of the logic in terms of clock generators and refresh logic.

APPLICATIONS

Shift registers are widely used in video terminals, communication buffers, and other systems where random access to specified data words is not required.

3.6   READ-ONLY MEMORY (ROM)

DESCRIPTION

ROM ICs are used to store binary information in a permanent pattern which is part of the manufacturing process. The binary bit pattern is retained in the ROM when power is removed from the IC, making it a nonvolatile memory.

The general ROM operation is described below and illustrated in Figure 3.6.

Write Operation: The user of the ROM defines the information to be programmed on a set of computer cards. This set of cards is sent to the manufacturer where the information is used to create a "mask" for the ROM. The "mask" is bonded for assembly for each ROM purchased.

Read Operation: The binary address lines are decoded by the address decode logic to select a specific memory location (word). The data stored in the memory location is connected to the data output buffers. When the chip select is activated, the data word is connected to the output data bus.

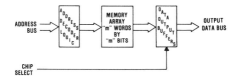

Figure 3.6. Read-Only Memory (ROM)

KEY PARAMETERS

a) *Address set-up time.* The time the system must wait before the data is valid on the output of the ROM IC. This assumes the chip select is activated. Set-up time ranges from 45 to 450 ns.

b) *Chip select set-up time.* The time the system must wait before the data is valid on the outputs of the ROM IC after the chip select is activated. This assumes the address bus is at the selected value. Values vary from 45 to 200 ns.

c) *Chip disable.* The time the system must wait for the ROM IC to deactivate its data buffers after the chip select is disabled. The range is 30 to 200 ns.

d) *Memory organization.* The structure of the ROM IC in terms of the number of words and the number of bits per word. The size of ROMs varies from 256 words by 4 bits to 4096 words by 8 bits.

APPLICATIONS

ROMs are used for storing control programs for computer control systems, calculators, look-up tables, character generation, code converters, etc.

COMMENTS

ROMs should be considered as alternatives to PROMs when used in large quantities because ROMs are generally less expensive than PROMs.

3.7 PROGRAMMABLE READ-ONLY MEMORY (PROM)

DESCRIPTION

In the programmable read-only memory (PROM), binary bit patterns are permanently entered into the memory device. The user can program the PROM IC to his particular bit pattern, while ROMs must be programmed by the manufacturer. Once programmed, the PROM is used only to read selected memory locations for the binary bit patterns contained in each word. Removing power from the IC does not destroy the bit patterns. The programming procedure for entering each memory word may vary from IC to the IC, but the original binary information is again available to the user. This feature makes it non-volatile. As illustrated in Figure 3.7, the PROM IC operates as follows:

Write Operation: The write operation can only be done once and the programming procedure for entering each memory word varies from IC to IC. In general, there are fusable links for each bit in the memory

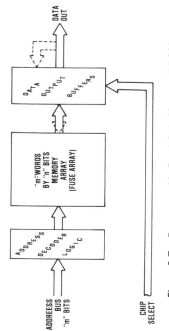

Figure 3.7. Programmable Read-Only Memory (PROM)

array. The address bus is set to the initial starting value of "0" and the address decode logic selects the first word in the memory array. Next, the chip select line is activated and each data output line is connected to a high-voltage, high-current device (HVHCD). The activation of each HVHCD is a function of whether or not 1's or 0's will be programmed into a particular bit in a memory location. As a general rule, the activation of the HVHCD will open the fusable link. Once the operation is completed, the next memory location is selected by changing the value on the address bus. The cycle is then repeated.

Read Operation: The binary value on the address bus to the PROM is decoded by the address decode logic. Each output of the decode logic is connected to a different memory location. Based on the way the given memory location was programmed, the selected bit pattern is connected to the data output buffers. If the chip select line to the PROM IC is activated, the binary value for the selected word is connected to the data out lines of the IC. If the chip select is not activated, the data-out lines are switched open, allowing other memory ICs to use the same data out lines.

KEY PARAMETERS

a) ***Read access time.*** The time from the beginning of the chip select and address lines to the time the data is to be read on the data output buffers. Minimum time requirement begins at 30 ns. If the address bus can be stabilized prior to activating the chip select line, the time to wait before the data is available at the outputs can be shortened.

b) *Chip disable time.* This parameter determines whether other memory ICs can take control of the data bus. The system must wait a finite period of time after the chip select signal is deactivated. The minimum time is 20 ns.

c) *Power dissipation.* The amount of power consumed by the PROM IC depends on the technology used in the structure of the chip, the speed at which the IC can operate, and whether or not special circuits are used to remove power to the IC when the memory is not chip selected. The power dissipation can range from 30 microwatts to 150 microwatts per bit of storage. To determine the power dissipation (PD) of the PROM IC use the following formula: PD = (# of bits for the PROM IC) times (PD for each bit.)

APPLICATIONS

PROMs are used in place of ROMs, wherever the number of devices is limited. The cost of mask-encoded ROMs is only warranted when thousands of identical ROMs are used. Most PROMs are used in mini- and microcomputers.

3.8 ELECTRICALLY ALTERABLE READ-ONLY MEMORY (EAROM)

DESCRIPTION

The EAROM IC illustrated in Figure 3.8 is designed to write, store and read binary information. EAROMs are non-volatile. Power can be removed and reapplied without any loss of the data stored in the memory array. Unlike the ROM and PROM, repeated write operations are possible. Data can be written, erased, and read electrically. The EAROM allows in-system modification of the binary bit patterns stored in the memory array, but the number of read and write operations is limited. Each time the read/write/erase operation occurs, the non-volatile storage life is reduced. The erase operation can erase one or all memory locations. The write/erase operation is slow, while the read operation can be done at high speed. Access to the data stored in the memory array is random. The binary value on the address bus selects the memory location for reading/writing/erasing. Multiple power supplies are required.

Write Operation: The activation of the selected output of the address decode logic is determined by the binary value on the address bus. When the chip select line is enabled, the data word is routed through the data I/O logic to the specified location in the memory array. When the write pulse is generated for the specified period of time, the data word is stored in the memory location. Damage to the EAROM can occur if the signal is on too long.

132

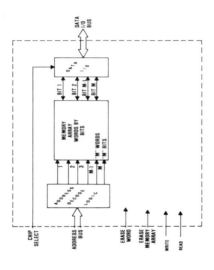

Figure 3.8.　Electrically Alterable Read-Only Memory (EAROM)

Erase Operation: This operation deletes the binary bit pattern in a specified memory location or in the whole memory array. The erase operation must precede the write operation. When the erase word input is activated for the specified period of time, the data stored in the selected location in the memory array is deleted. If the erase memory array input is activated for the specified period of time, the contents of all memory locations are deleted. Exceeding the specified period of time for the erase operation can result in damage to the EAROM.

Read Operation: The read feature is similar in operation to other memory ICs. Which data word is read out of memory is determined by the binary value on the address bus. If the chip select is enabled, the data stored in the specific word is connected to the data I/O bus.

KEY PARAMETERS

a) *Erase time.* The time required to delete the binary bit pattern in the specified memory location or in the whole memory array. This time is approximately 14 ms. Exceeding the manufacturer's time limit can result in damage to the EAROM.

b) *Write time.* The time required to write a data word into a specified memory location. The approximate value is 2 ms. Exceeding the manufacturer's time limit can result in damage to the EAROM.

c) *Read access time.* The time required until data is available at the data I/O bus, once the address bus and chip select lines are activated. This time varies among different manufacturers. The range is 0.5 to 12 μs.

d) *Life of EAROM.* The guaranteed life of the memory array is determined by the number of erase/write and read operations.

Typical values are:

erase/write operations:100 operations
per word
read operation: several hundred
billions operation

e) *Power supplies.* Most EAROMs require multiple power supplies. The ranges of power-supply voltages are ±5V, ±12V, ±26V, etc.

APPLICATIONS

Whenever non-volatility is required. The storage of data, parameters or tables, where the values must be maintained during power failures at turn-off, is a suitable application of the EAROM. Due to the limitation of the number of erase/write/read operations, it is not suitable for applications where the read/write cycles are occurring frequently.

COMMENTS

The use of the EAROM in microprocessors is limited, except as a non-volatile storage device where its contents are transferred to a RAM. The system must be designed to execute the control program from the RAM rather than the EAROM.

The timing requirements for the erase and write operations are critical. Generally, a sequence control timing generation is used to supply the erase/write/read signals to the EAROM. Activation of the sequence would be controlled by the microprocessor or computer system.

3.9 ELECTRICALLY PROGRAMMABLE READ-ONLY MEMORY (EPROM)

DESCRIPTION

The EPROM is a non-volatile memory IC which is used to store binary information. Power can be removed without loss of data. Upon reapplying the power, the original binary data is still retained. Special circuits must be used to program the binary information into the memory array. This write function is done outside the system. Once programmed, the EPROM is placed back into the system and activated. One feature of the EPROM is that it can be reprogrammed to a new binary bit pattern. This is accomplished by exposing the EPROM to an ultra-violet (UV) source in order to erase the old binary information. A UV transparent lid on the chip allows this erasure to occur (page 138). Figure 3.9 defines the operation (page 138).

Erasure: In order to erase the EPROM, the UV transparent lid must be exposed to a UV source for approximately 10 to 20 minutes.

Write Operation: First the chip select line is deactivated in order to switch the data outputs to inputs. The address inputs are set to a starting value and the desired data word is connected to the data inputs of the EPROM. The program pin is then enabled. During the time of the program pulse, the data is written into the selected location of the memory array. This cycle is repeated for each location.

Read Operation: The read operation is similar to that used for RAMs, ROMs, PROMs, etc. The memory location, selected by the memory decode logic, is determined by the binary value on the address inputs. The data programmed in the memory array is connected to the data output buffers. If the chip select is activated, the data word is connected to the data bus. The data outputs are in the off-state when the chip select is disabled.

KEY PARAMETERS

a) *Program pulse.* The program pulse writes the data word into the selected memory location. It must be held active between 100 ms to 3 ms.
b) *Address set-up time.* The period of time the system must wait for the data to be valid on the data output lines. This assumes the chip select is activated. The range is 300 to 700 ns.
c) *Chip select time.* The period of time the system must wait for the data to be valid at the data output lines. This assumes the address lines are at the

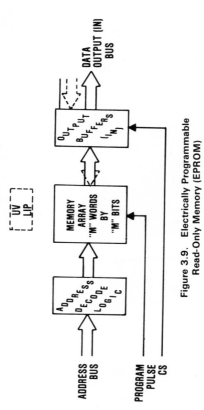

Figure 3.9. Electrically Programmable
Read-Only Memory (EPROM)

desired value. Typical delays are 100 to 175 ns.

d) *Output disable*. The time the system must wait for the data output lines of the EPROM to be deactivated once the chip select is disabled. This time ranges from 120 to 400 ns.

APPLICATIONS

The EPROM is used when the binary bit patterns are changed periodically. Look-up tables which are not the same from system to system are an example. Each table type must be programmed into a different EPROM. The EPROM is also used in microprocessor applications where the control program (set of instructions) is stored.

COMMENTS

EPROMs are temporarily used for the debugging of the control programs in the microprocessors. Once the program is debugged, the EPROMs are replaced with the less expensive ROMs or PROMs.

Chapter 4

Chapter Four is devoted to microcomputer and microprocessor ICs, one of the most rapidly growing fields of electronics. Since many of our readers are not familiar with all of the features of microcomputers and microprocessors we strongly urge you to read Section 4.1 below which provides the essential key definitions that apply to the entire field. Specific examples of two different microcomputers, three microprocessors and one microprocessor slice are included in this chapter. The information on these devices is necessarily concise, but is completely applicable to practically any other microcomputer, microprocessor or microprocessor slice currently in production. Minor differences of internal architecture generally do not affect the key parameters described in this chapter.

4.1 MICROCOMPUTER AND MICROPROCESSOR ICs

DESCRIPTION

The block diagram of Figure 4.1 shows the key elements of any digital computer.

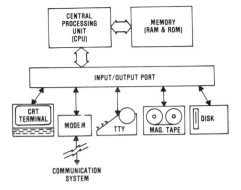

Figure 4.1. Computer Block Diagram

Recent advances in large-scale integrated (LSI) ICs have made it possible to provide the central processing unit (CPU), the RAM and ROM memory and the input/output (I/O) port functions on a single IC. The capabilities of such a microcomputer (MC) are not as extensive as those of a computer consisting of a large number of ICs, but the essential functions are the same. When only the CPU is contained on a single IC, more capabilities become available and this microprocessor (MP) can be combined with memory and other digital ICs to approach the capabilities of a minicomputer. A microprocessor slice contains only some of the functions of a CPU, but performs those functions faster.

Like all digital computers, MCs and MPs perform certain binary functions according to the instructions contained in the control program. This program (software)

141

is stored in some memory section, in binary form, and determines just what the CPU, or MP, does with the data, which is stored in another memory section. All of the functions of the MC and the MP are designed to move, decode, and execute the instructions contained in the control program and manipulate the data accordingly. Both the program and the data must be entered, at some time, from an external device (peripheral).

MCs and MPs are often classified according to the number of parallel binary bits they can handle. Standard sizes are the 4-bit, 8-bit, and 16-bit systems, and compatibility with bus (Interconnection) systems having the respective number of parallel lines is essential. The greater the number of bits, the more powerful, and expensive, will be the entire computer system. Clearly a device able to handle four bits as address can address only 16 locations, while an 8-bit device can address 256 locations, at the same time, with the same clock frequency. Detailed descriptions concerning instructions, memory addressing, and other features will be found in the manufacturer's literature.

Hardware Configuration: ICs are available that perform all or part of the different computer functions. As illustrated in Figure 4.01, we can identify three basic categories:

1. *Microcomputer ICs*. These ICs contain all the functions of a computer system, including the EPROM, ROM, and RAM for storing the control program and data words to be processed. The controller and arith-

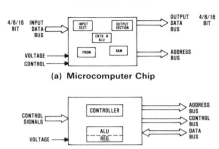

(a) Microcomputer Chip

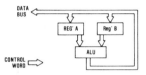

(b) Microprocessor Chip

(c) Processor-Slice Chip

Figure 4.01. (a) Microcomputer Chip
(b) Microprocessor Chip
(c) Processor-Slice Chip

metic logic unit (ALU) are the brains, while the input and output (I/O) sections are used to transfer information over the two data buses. The control program is limited by the size of the EPROM or ROM inside the IC, but some microcomputer ICs provide external memory expansion features, including an address bus.

An important characteristic of any microcomputer is the size of the data word that can be processed. There are 4, 8, and 16-bit microcomputer ICs. The number of bits

143

determines the maximum value of the word that can be processed at any given time. For example, an "add" instruction executed by a 4-bit computer can add values up to 16, but with an 8-bit microcomputer values up to 256 can be added. (See Figure 4.01(a)).

2. *Microprocessor ICs*. This IC is used where larger control programs and greater flexibility are needed. As illustrated in Figure 4.01(b), the microprocessor contains no memory, but performs the key functions of the arithmetic logic unit (ALU) and the controller. It also contains a set of internal registers and I/O ports to communicate with external computer elements. The address and data bus is used to access specific locations in the external memory during the "fetch" cycle. The ALU and register section is used to manipulate and provide temporary storage for the data words. Microprocessor ICs are available in 4, 8, and 16-bit versions, with 32-bit units expected in the early 1980s.

3. *Slice Processor ICs*. In many applications, flexibility and speed are the dominant considerations in the design of the system. Slice processor ICs are used when the number of ICs and cost are not important. The only function contained in this type of IC is the arithmetic logic unit (ALU) and some registers to temporarily store the data words, as shown in Figure 4.01(c). The controller, memory elements, and all other control functions must be provided external to the slice processor ICs. An external control word is used to select which register contains the data words to be processed and the type of function the ALU will perform on the data words. Slice processor ICs are

available in 2, 4 and 8-bit slices. They can be cascaded for 8, 12, 16, 32-bit systems.

4.2 8-BIT MICROCOMPUTER

DESCRIPTION

The 8-bit microcomputer illustrated in Figure 4.2 is a complete computer system contained on a single IC. It contains a ROM/EPROM, RAM and a microprocessor, including the controller, program control, ALU and some registers. Using the 8-bit microcomputer rather than a 4-bit microcomputer allows the control program to be written with fewer instructions. Furthermore, larger numbers can be processed with the 8-bit microcomputer IC.

The control program, once written and debugged, is programmed into the ROM or EPROM. If a ROM microcomputer IC is used, the programming must be done by the manufacturer. If an EPROM is used, the programming is done at the user's facility. The decision as to which type to use is based on speed, cost, flexibility, etc. (See Chapter 3 on EPROM or ROMs.)

When power is applied, the reset line is activated, causing the controller to clear the program counter. The first instruction is read from the **0** address of the ROM or EPROM to the instruction register where it is decoded and executed. The following types of instructions are available to the user. Arithmetic and logic instructions are used in conjunction with the internal RAM, accumulator, and arithmetic logic unit. Input or output instructions, written in the

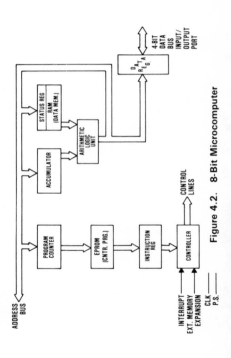

Figure 4.2. 8-Bit Microcomputer

146

control program, transfer data words between the accumulator or RAM and the input/output port of the microcomputer. The balance of the instructions in the instruction set are used for manipulating the control counter. The interrupt steers the microcomputer to a different section of the control program. Provisions are included for external memory expansion.

KEY PARAMETERS

a) *EPROM/ROM size.* The maximum size of the control program that can be programmed into the EPROM/ROM. The size varies from 256 to 2048 locations. (Note: External memory expansion increases the size.)

b) *RAM size.* The maximum number of internal memory locations used to temporarily store information. The size varies from 16 to 128 locations.

c) *Interrupt.* 1 to 6 interrupts are available with the present 8-bit microcomputers.

d) *Instruction set.* The number of instructions varies from 30 to 102 instructions.

e) *Clock.* The speed of the clock combined with the numbers of clock cycles per instruction determines the execute time of the microcomputer.

APPLICATIONS

As with the 4, 8, 16-bit microprocessors and 4-bit microcomputer, the 8-bit microcomputer can be used in microwave ovens, TV games, calculators, etc.

COMMENTS

Additional functions are included in some microcomputers. These functions include timers, UARTS, etc. The timer is provided to generate a real time clock and the UART permits serial data transfers.

4.3   4-BIT MICROCOMPUTER

DESCRIPTION

The 4-bit microcomputer illustrated in Figure 4.3 is a complete computer system contained in a single IC. This computer system contains a ROM which stores the control program that is designed to perform a specific function. In addition, a RAM is included for temporary storage of data. The ALU and the associated logic elements execute instructions from the control program. The 4-bit microcomputer operates with the following two major cycles:

a) *Fetch Cycle*. When the microcomputer is in this mode, the location of the ROM specified by the program control is read into the instruction register. Upon completion of this cycle the computer enters the execute cycle.

b) *Execute Cycle*. In this cycle the instruction stored in the instruction register is executed by the controller. If it was an add instruction, the binary word stored in the accumulator is added to the contents of the specified location. In addition, the status

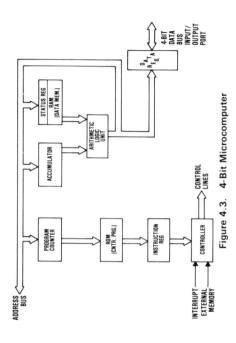

Figure 4.3. 4-Bit Microcomputer

149

register is updated. If an output or input instruction is executed, a 4-bit data transfer occurs between the input/output data port and the accumulator or a specified location in the RAM.

KEY PARAMETERS

a) *Control program size.* The number of instructions stored in the internal ROM varies from 256 to 2048 instructions.
b) *Interrupt.* In most microcomputers either 0, 1, or 2 interrupts are allowed.
c) *Instruction set.* The number of basic instructions varies from 3 to 74 instructions.
d) *Clock.* Different microcomputers operate at a clock frequency from 300 kHz to 5.0 MHz.
e) *Internal storage locations.* The number of RAM locations varies from 16 to 160 words.

APPLICATIONS

The 4-bit microcomputer is used where simple dedicated functions will be performed. Cash registers, TV games, microwave ovens, are typical consumer products that use this IC.

COMMENTS

Consideration must be given to the size of the control program when using the 4-bit microcomputer. The size of the program is limited to the size of the internal ROM.

Many of the 4-bit microcomputers do not have the capability to expand the ROM by adding external ICs. If the size of the control program exceeds the size of the internal ROM, the 4-bit microcomputer cannot be used.

4.4 16-BIT MICROPROCESSOR (MP)

DESCRIPTION:

The 16-bit microprocessor illustrated in Figure 4.4 is similar in structure to the 4 and 8-bit microprocessor, but there are some differences:

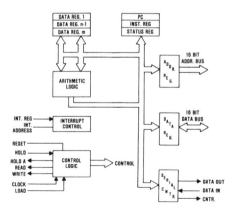

Figure 4.4. 16-Bit Microprocessor

a) Larger numbers can be manipulated within a single instruction cycle. Numeric values up to 65 thousand can be processed in one add cycle, while the 8-bit microprocessor is limited to numeric values up to 256 in one add cycle.

b) Fetch cycles are required in most instructions, but in the 8-bit MP two fetch cycles are required to read a 16-bit instruction.

c) The latest digital design techniques such as "memory to memory operations," "instruction queue," are used with 16-bit microprocessor, permitting faster execution times of the control program.

The operation of the microprocessor is characterized by the major cycles described below:

Fetch Cycle. During the fetch cycle the binary value stored in the program counter (PC) is routed through the 16-bit address register to the address bus. The PC contains the address of the instruction being executed at the present time. The address register stores the address long enough to access the external memory storing the control program. The binary value on the address bus is decoded by the memory IC in order to read the selected instruction onto the 16-bit data bus. This instruction is processed through the data register and written into the instruction register. The control logic generates all necessary timing signals for this cycle to occur.

Execute Cycle. When in the execute cycle, the control logic generates the necessary signals to perform the instruction. If an add instruction is being executed, the arithmetic logic unit (ALU) would be set to the ADD function. Other command signals from the control logic connect the selected registers to the ALU. Once the add function is completed, the result of the addition is written into one of the internal registers in the MP or a location in the external memory chip. The number of internal data registers varies between different microprocessor types, but some have no internal registers. In these ICs, memory address data registers are used. These MADRs are assigned locations in the external memory ICs. The memory location is determined by the instruction and the contents of an internal register which defines the starting address. Completion of certain types of instructions can result in flag bits being set in the status register. The status register consists of storage elements which are used by the control program. These storage elements indicate certain events that might have occurred during the execution of the instructions.

Interrupt Control. The interrupt control block is able to take control of the microprocessor and steer it to another part of the control program if certain events external to the MP have occurred. The decision to allow the interrupt to take control is selectable by the control program, and the number of different interrupts available varies between microprocessor models. If there is more than one interrupt, an interrupt request (Int Req) and interrupt address register are included in the MP.

Once an interrupt occurs, the control logic stops what it is doing at the end of the present execute cycle. The control logic then generates the appropriate command signals which save the contents of the program counter, status register and the "data registers." This allows the microprocessor to return to its original program upon completion of the interrupt program. Once the information is saved in memory, the MP switches to a designated memory location, based on the interrupt value. The contents of the memory location define the starting location of the interrupt program.

Serial Control. Certain 16-bit microprocessors have, in addition to a parallel interface, a serial interface to the I/O. This control line is pulsed each time a data bit is sent. The decision to activate the serial control logic is determined by a program instruction.

in addition to these major cycles, most MPs also operate on a series of special control signals.

KEY PARAMETERS

a) *Direct addressing.* The number of locations that can be accessed directly by the microprocessor. From 32K words to 14 M bytes.

b) *Hardware interrupts.* The number of interrupts permitted in a particular microprocessor. The number ranges from 16 to 256 interrupts.

c) *Instruction set.* The number of instructions that the microprocessor executes. This varies from 33 to 153 instructions.

d) *Clock.* The highest frequency at which the microprocessor will operate. 2.0 to 14.0 MHz is typical.

e) *Internal registers.* Internal registers available to manipulate the data. They range from none up to 16.

APPLICATIONS

16-bit microprocessor MPs will provide faster throughput than 4- and 8-bit microprocessors. Present applications include TV games, airborne control systems, process control applications, personal computers and small business computers.

4.5 8-BIT MICROPROCESSOR (MP)

DESCRIPTION

The 8-bit microprocessor illustrated in Figure 4.5 acts as controller in a microcomputer system. An 8-bit MP provides faster execution times and higher performances than a 4-bit MP. A 4-bit MP would require more than one add instruction when adding numbers greater than 16, but an 8-bit MP can handle numbers up to 256. The fetch and execute cycles of the 8-bit MP are essentially the same as described in 4.4 for the 16-bit MP.

In addition to the fetch and execute cycle, the following control functions are included in most 8 and 16-bit microprocessors:

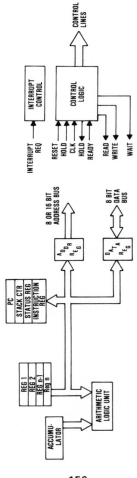

Figure 4.5. 8-Bit Microprocessor

156

Reset Signal: All control programs have a starting point when power is applied. As a general guide, the starting address is location 0. When the input reset line is activated, the MP resets the program counter to "0" and enters a fetch cycle. Information from location 0 of the external memory is read into the microprocessor and executed. This information could represent a linking address to another section of the control program or an instruction.

Load Signal: The load signal operates in a similar fashion to the reset signal. The load signal is used to force the MP to another section of the control program. When the load input is activated, the program counter (PC) is set to a specific value and connected to the address bus. The value on the address bus is used to specify the memory location to be read back into the PC.

Based on the design of the specific MP, this information is used as a link or starting address for the program.

Hold/Hold A: These signals are used to stop the MP from executing the control program in order to execute direct memory access (DMA) transfer. The DMA operation transfers binary information between the memory and other parts of the system. DMA is used because the MP cannot operate at the speeds required by the incoming data, such as information from a disc or a high-speed data link. Activation of a DMA transfer occurs when the hold signal is applied. The MP stops at the end of the next memory cycle and puts the address and data bus, write and read lines into a high impedance state. This allows the DMA controller to utilize these lines without interference from the MP. The DMA data and address word is then connected to the memory bus and a write signal is generated.

Stack: This section of the MP is used to store the address of routines which have been interrupted until the interrupt is completed.

KEY PARAMETERS

  a) *Direct addressing.* The number of memory locations directly accessible by the MP. This varies from 2K bytes to 128K bytes.
  b) *Interrupts.* 8-bit MPs have interrupt requests but no provisions to process multiple interrupts. (See Section 4.4.) External hardware must be included in the system to provide a multiple interrupt function.
  c) *Instruction set.* The number of instructions goes from 8 to 96.
  d) *Clock.* The highest frequency at which the MP operates. For 8-bit microprocessors the maximum is between 2 and 10 MHz.
  e) *Internal registers.* The number of general purpose registers available within the MP. They vary from 0 to 128.

APPLICATIONS

8-bit MPs are used in the majority of microcomputer systems on the market. They find application in electronic games, ap-

pliance controls, personal computers, auto-
motive controls, and industrial controls.

4.6 4-BIT
MICROPROCESSOR (MP)

DESCRIPTION

The 4-bit microprocessor illustrated in
Figure 4.6 is used to process binary and
BCD information. This MP has two basic
cycles, fetch and execute. While in the fetch
cycle, the binary value in the program
counter (PC) is connected to the 12-bit address bus and a read command is generated
from the control logic. During the read
command, the instruction stored in the
location specified by the information on the
address bus is read via the data bus into the
data register. This information is then
transferred to the instruction register. The
MP then enters the execute cycle.

In the execute cycle the instruction is
decoded and the appropriate commands
generated. If an add instruction is to be
executed, a command from the control logic
connects the selected register to the arithmetic logic unit (ALU). The ALU is set up to
perform an add function between the binary
information in the accumulator and the
selected register. The result of the addition
is then transferred into the accumulator
and the previous information stored in the
accumulator is destroyed. If the resultant
number is too large for the accumulator, the
appropriate flag bits in the status register
are set. The status register is used to store
events such as overflow, equal, etc.—events

159

Figure 4.6. 4-Bit Microprocessor

160

that occurred as a result of executing the instruction. The flag bits set can be tested by succeeding instructions.

Another function provided in the MP is the interrupt. If the interrupt line is activated, the MP stops what it is doing and proceeds to a different section of the control program. The ready and wait signals are used when the MP is working with memory elements which are slower in speed. The memory section of the system is designed so that whenever the read or write signal is activated, the ready line to the MC is pulled down. This causes the MP to stop whatever it is doing and allows the memory elements to respond to the information on the address and data bus. During this time the wait signal from the MP is generated. Once the memory elements perform the read or write operation, the ready line is deactivated. allowing the MP to continue in the control program.

KEY PARAMETERS

a) *Direct addressing.* The number of memory locations that can be directly accessed by the microprocessor. These locations can be used to store instructions or data. The number of locations varies from 4K to 8K words.

b) *Interrupts.* The number of interrupts that direct the MP to execute a different set of instructions. As a general rule there are from 1 to 8 interrupts.

c) *Instruction set.* The number of different instructions that can be executed by the MP. This number varies from 16 to 64 instructions.

d) *Clock.* The speed at which the microprocessor operates. Note: Multiple clock cycles are required to execute a single instruction. The clock frequency varies from 0.5 to 2 MHz.

e) *Internal register.* The number of registers which can be used to store binary information. This number can vary from 1 to 24 registers.

APPLICATIONS

The 4-bit MP is used in slow speed, simply controlled consumer products, such as microwave ovens, TV games, etc.

4.7 4-BIT MICROPROCESSOR SLICE (MPS)

The 4-bit microprocessor slice illustrated in Figure 4.7 performs the basic function of arithmetic, logic, and data manipulation operations. This is different in operation from regular MPs which not only perform the above operation but also supply all timing signals necessary to execute a control program. Regular MPs are designed for the additional feature and are slower for a given program than the MP slice which only operates on the data and does not supply the control signals for the entire system.

The MP slice is under the control of an external control word, which consists of two parts—the address and the operand. The address part of the word is connected to the address bus, while the operand word controls the arithmetic logic unit.

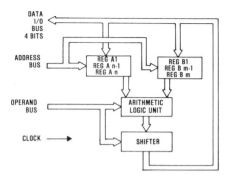

Figure 4.7.   4-Bit Microprocessor Slice

The address bus is activated in order to select the registers to read or write the data words. If data is in the register, the operand bus is used to select one of the functions designed into the ALU, such as add, subtract, complement, etc. If the data is to be shifted left or right, the appropriate code is sent to the shifter logic. The control word, consisting of the operand and address, is sent to the MP slice where it is then executed. If data is to be transferred between the MP slice and the external hardware, the data I/O bus is activated. The control words are stored in an external memory such as a PROM or ROM and executed sequentially.

KEY PARAMETERS

a) *Number of basic instructions (Operand Code).* Which instruction is

163

executed by the MP slice is determined by the external control word. Their number varies from 8 to 42 instructions.

b) *Number of internal registers.* The number of registers used to store data varies from 0 to 20. In the case where no registers are included in the MP slice, external registers are designed into the system.

c) *Address bus.* The address bus for the MP slice relates specifically to the number of internal registers. The bus size varies from 0 to 4 bits.

d) *Clock.* The rate at which the MP slice will execute an instruction. The rate varies from 5 to 20 MHz.

APPLICATIONS

The MP slice is used in applications where speed is the primary consideration in the design of the system. Cost and IC density would be a secondary consideration. MP slice systems are used in dedicated applications where through-put is important.

COMMENTS

MP slice ICs really execute micro-instructions. An add instruction might require five to ten micro-instructions and a specific sequence is required to generate the ten micro-instructions. The sequence generation is external to the MP slice. To perform multi-bit operations, several 4-bit MPs slice must be cascaded. To execute a 16-bit add instruction, four 4-bit MPs slice must be used.

Chapter 5

The range of microprocessor/microcomputer support functions continues to grow, as the more or less standardized microprocessors and microcomputers themselves are used in an ever-growing range of applications. Many of these applications require specific support functions for which manufacturers design and produce separate ICs. Following a brief discussion of support functions in general, we present five different ICs which are typical of the most widely used support function ICs. While most microprocessors and microcomputers contain a clock generator as part of the IC, this is usually insufficient for larger systems involving other elements than the basic parts of a microcomputer. For this reason, microprocessor clock generators are widely available. The I/O function of most microprocessors and computers also needs expansion and a typical IC to perform this function is included here. The interrupt controller provides a hardware means to perform a function which can often also be performed by software, but usually at much greater cost. A typical interval timer for microprocessors and microcomputers is included here, as well as a programmable interface. This last IC allows the computer designer a great deal of flexibility in the total computer architecture and a number of different devices of this type are used with different systems.

As in all preceding chapters, the material presented here is intended to provide key quick-reference data and cannot be expected to take the place of detailed manufacturer's technical data in the case of a new design effort or a detailed circuit analysis.

5.1 MICROPROCESSOR/ MICROCOMPUTER SUPPORT FUNCTIONS

DESCRIPTION

Neither the microprocessor (MP) nor the microcomputer (MC) ICs described in Chapter 4 forms a complete system. Both must be connected to peripheral devices, to additional memory, and to some very specialized support ICs. The interface ICs for external memory devices and for other peripherals are included in the Vestpocket Handbook on Interface ICs.

The specialized MP and MC support ICs described in this section are representative examples of the most widely used types. In general, a particular MP or MC family includes a variety of support ICs, tailored to the MP and MC and configured for specific applications. In some instances two or more support functions are included in one IC. The clock generator and interrupt controller are functions that almost every MP and MC requires. The programmable interface and the I/O expansion are also frequently required, but the interval time is not always used, since its function can be implemented by the program. Interval timers are very popular for personal computers where home appliance control is an important feature.

KEY PARAMETERS

Support ICs are generally applicable only to the MP and MC families for which they are designed. Their key parameters will therefore be the same as for the particular MP or MC. Specific function parameters are listed in the following pages for each IC.

APPLICATIONS

Support ICs are used with the particular MP or MC for which they are designed as part of the total computer system.

5.2 MICROPROCESSOR CLOCK GENERATOR

DESCRIPTION

Many manufacturers of microprocessors (MP) provide an associated clock generator IC capable of generating the proper timing signals for the MP.

Figure 5.2 is the block diagram of an MP clock generator IC and shows a crystal connected to the oscillator input of the clock generator. A crystal is used to insure accuracy and stability. The frequency divider establishes the actual clock frequency of the MP and determines the duty cycle for the clock, such as 25% on, 75% off. This duty cycle allows the phasing of the clocks to be developed and minimizes noise to the MP. The output of the frequency divider is connected both to the phase generator and to the decoder. The phase generator sets up the timing as to when each clock output will be activated. Correct phasing of the clock is important since the MP performs certain basic functions at each phase. In a fetch cycle, for example, phase 1 sets the address bus to a memory location. Phase 2 might start the read or write signal. Phase 3 might be used to start the data transfer between the MP and the memory element.

The decoder logic is used to gate the clock from the frequency divider into the individual phases, and the number of decoder gates depends on the number of clock phases required. The drivers set the clock signals to the correct voltage levels.

KEY PARAMETERS

a) *Frequency.* Defines the frequency of the basic clock cycle. The frequency can be as high as 50.0 MHz.
b) *Phase.* The number of clock outputs from the clock generator IC. It varies between one and four clock outputs.
c) *Voltage level.* The voltage levels range from −12 to +18 volts.

APPLICATIONS

The clock generator IC is usually designed to interface with a particular microprocessor family.

COMMENTS

Microprocessor ICs are usually TTL compatible for the address and data bus, but the clock inputs are not. Some clock generator ICs include additional functions such as the reset, load or interrupt signals.

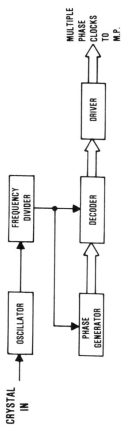

Figure 5.2. Microprocessor Clock Generator

169

5.3 MICROCOMPUTER INPUT/OUTPUT EXPANDER

DESCRIPTION

This IC is used with microcomputers (MC) to increase the number of data ports and allows the MC to interface with additional peripheral devices such as keyboards, printers, modems, etc. Figure 5.3 represents the typical block diagram for this IC. The width of the data port may range from 4 to 16 bits. Specific instructions in the computer program control access to the IC expander, including an address field which determines the I/O port that will be used.

The address decoder generates the appropriate command signals to the selected port. When a "read I/O" instruction occurs, the data word on the selected input buffer is routed through the multiplexer to the external data bus to the MC. If the I/O instruction is a "write," the data word is transferred from the MC over the data bus through the demultiplexer to the latch of the selected port.

KEY PARAMETERS

a) *Port width.* The number of bits must be the same as in the MC.

b) *Number of ports.* The user assigns each port to a peripheral device. Most I/O expanders have four ports.

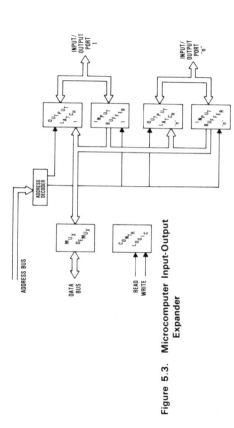

Figure 5.3. Microcomputer Input-Output
Expander

171

APPLICATIONS

I/O expanders are used in microcomputer systems when the number of peripherals is greater than the number of ports available in the MC itself.

5.4   INTERRUPT CONTROLLER

DESCRIPTION

Interrupt controller ICs are designed to process and format the interrupt requests generated by the various peripheral devices such as keyboards, timers, printers, etc. Interrupt requests are then sent to the microprocessor (MP) or microcomputer (MC). These interrupt requests are used to steer the MP or MC to a different part of the control program, enabling the system to handle the various "real time" requests occurring periodically from peripheral devices. Figure 5.4 represents a typical functional block diagram of an interrupt controller IC. Interrupt requests are received from the various peripheral devices in the total system.

When the operator depresses a key on the keyboard, for example, the assigned interrupt request is activated. This request is routed through the interrupt buffer to the masking gates. The masking gates are used to prevent selected interrupt requests from being processed. There are times when the MP or MC executes sections of the control program which cannot tolerate an interrupt request. In order to prevent these requests

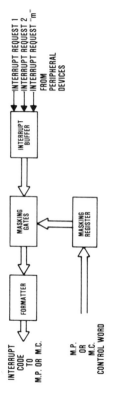

Figure 5.4. Interrupt Controller

173

from being processed, the MP or MC will generate a control word which is sent to the interrupt controller over the control word bus. This control word is stored in the masking register. Each bit in the control word is assigned to an interrupt input. If the bit is set, the interrupt masking latch is enabled, causing the masking gate to inhibit any requests for that input. If the masking bit is disabled the interrupt request line is enabled, allowing any interrupt request to be processed by the MP or MC. The formatter encodes the interrupt request and generates the control signals sent to the MP or MC. This is done to minimize the number of interrupt control lines.

KEY PARAMETERS

a) *Number of interrupts*. The number of interrupts varies from one to as many as 16.

APPLICATIONS

Interrupt controllers are used wherever MCs or MPs are working with peripheral devices requiring real time service.

COMMENTS

Depending on the MP or MCs used, the interrupt/address select logic is either internal or must be supplied by external logic. The interrupt address select logic activates a different starting address on the address bus for each interrupt. Polling is another method used to determine when a peripheral device requires servicing. It is less expensive to implement in hardware, but more time consuming.

5.5 INTERVAL TIMER

DESCRIPTION

The interval timer, as illustrated in Figure 5.5, consists of binary or BCD counters, connected to an external clock and the microprocessor (MP) or computer (MC). The external clock is usually an accurate and stable pulse train at a specific frequency. For each clock pulse the counter advances by one bit and generates one output pulse at a predetermined value. This predetermined value is established by the MP or MC. In a typical example an interrupt is required every two ms. In order to set up the two ms interrupt, a binary word from the MP or MC is transferred over the data bus and the data buffers to the selected counter. The particular counter is selected by the information on the address bus. The value of the binary information word is based on the frequency of the clock and the number of bits in the counter. The output pulse line is connected to an interrupt controller as described in 5.4.

The following calculation shows how the predetermined value of the data word sent to the counter is obtained:

If a clock frequency of 1 MHz and an interval time of two ms is assumed, the least

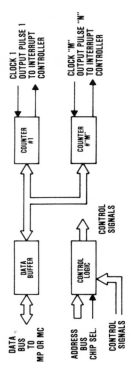

Figure 5.5. Interval Timer

significant bit has a decimal value of one ms, bit #2 will be two ms, bit #3 will be four ms, etc.

Using the decimal-to-binary conversion procedure, the binary word is 011111010000. This binary word is complemented and sent to the selected counter.

KEY PARAMETERS

a) *Number of counters.* Each counter in the interval timer can be used for a different time value. Interval timers are available with as many as four separate counters.

b) *Number of bits per counter.* The size of the counter and the frequency of the external clock determine the maximum time entered. Counter lengths vary from 8 to 16 bits.

c) *Speed of operation.* The maximum allowable clock frequency determines the accuracy, resolution, and smallest time internal. Clock frequencies of up to 3.0 MHz are typical.

APPLICATIONS

Used in computer based systems where real time processing is required. Microwave ovens and TV games are typical examples.

COMMENTS

All characteristics of the interval timer are programmable and this function can be achieved by software. While most of the counters are straight binary, there are some interval timers that provide binary-coded decimal (BCD) operation.

5.6 MICROPROCESSOR PROGRAMMABLE INTERFACE

DESCRIPTION

Most microprocessors (MP) provide only one data and address bus, which operate at the speed of the microprocessor. There are many applications where the peripheral devices connected to the MP must operate at different speeds. In addition, the size of the data word may vary between particular peripherals. The programmable interface can be used to increase the number of interfaces and accommodate different word lengths and data rates. As illustrated in the block diagram of Figure 5.6, instructions in the control program determine which port is selected for a data transfer. Data words can be transferred either from the MP to the selected port or from the selected port to the MP. In addition, ports can be assigned to a communications channel, video display, keyboard, etc.

When a "write I/O" instruction is executed, the data word from the MP is placed on the data bus to the programmable interface. The binary word on the address bus defines which activated port will receive the data. When the write signal is received, internal control signals are generated, caus-

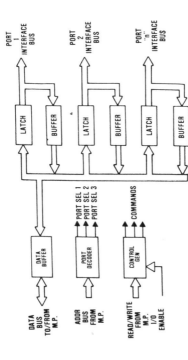

Figure 5.6. Programmable Interface IC

179

ing the data word to be loaded into the selected latch. The interface bus for the selected port will be configured for the data word from the MP. When data is transferred to the MP it sends a "read I/O" instruction. The number of the selected port is sent out over the address bus to the port decoder. When the read and I/O enable signals are activated, the information on the selected port interface bus is routed through the input data buffers over the internal data bus through the main data buffers to the MP. Each port is bidirectional, i.e., it can be programmed as an input or output port.

KEY PARAMETERS

a) *Number of ports.* The number of ports varies from one to four.
b) *Number of bits per port.* The size of the port, in bits, is often the same as the MP. Port sizes range from 4 to 16 bits.

APPLICATIONS

This IC extends the I/O capability of MPs.

COMMENTS

Programmable interface ICs can also include other features such as interrupt controller, interval timers, etc. In some of these ICs an individual bit can be programmed for both sending and receiving data bits.

INDEX

183